the near end of god

the
near
end
of
god

Not a distant deity...our loving God
...close, warm, ready to help, a powerful Friend.

richard angell

Pleasant W rd
A Division of WINEPRESS PUBLISHING

Dedication

To my parents—
For my mother, Evalyn Wells Angell, Phi Beta Kappa writer of reviews, articles, lover of books, founder of literary societies, literacy programs, and family prayer warrior. My dad, a great storyteller, would embellish personal anecdotes for the sake of the story; they were great and funny. My mom would roll her eyes and say some day she was going to write a book called "The *Real* Story." I wish she had. It would have been funny, too.

For my father, Dr. Warren M. Angell, composer, performer, author, teacher, musician, conductor, and creative artist, who believes that "Everything I'm doing now is just preparation for what I will be doing" (spoken at age 76 or thereabouts; now age 98 and looking ahead to new projects).

With great affection and love. My sisters and I had a heckuva good time growing up. I wish we had realized it at the time.

Special
Acknowledgment

A simple thank you is not adequate for the invaluable assistance of Vicki Coates, an insightful and knowledgeable editor with a whim of steel, computer wizard, and a special leader of the "balcony people," without whom this book would never have seen the light of day because I hate computers and write too many long sentences even though at times I write real good...

Minister Harry Emerson Fosdick had a cabin off the coast of Maine where he usually spent his summers. He once said in a sermon that he had never sailed the seven seas—the vast oceans of the world—but he knew something about them because of the near end of it that washed the shores around the island. So he said we may think of the place of Jesus in our faith. He is the man who presents God to us as no other does. He is the one who brings the near end of God to our doorstep.

—James Bortello, *About and for God*

God can be thought of as Absolute Being; He is that. But in a crisis—where a man grapples with an unmanageable habit, or an abysmal grief—an Absolute Being can be as distant, cold, and useless as the man in the moon. *What we need in a crisis is the near end of God:* God as we understand Him, God as an available resource close at hand, our unseen friend, our invisible companion.

—Harry Emerson Fosdick, *Those Marvelous Twelve Steps*

Fosdick says it is this way with God. He is so great, that in His vastness, we can only glimpse a little of His glory and sometimes that frightens us. But God also has a near-end that touches us and can be touched by us. To Christians that near-end of God is Jesus. *When we see God revealed in Jesus we are not frightened by His greatness, we are captivated by His dearness....*

—J. A. Lavender, *Project Winsome International*

How good it would be if we could learn that God is easy to live with... God is the sum of all patience and the essence of kindly good will. We please Him most, not by frantically trying to make ourselves good, but by throwing ourselves into His arms with all our imperfections, and believing that He understands everything and loves us still.

—A. W. Tozer, *The Root of the Righteous*

"To behold and gaze upon the beauty [the sweet attractiveness and delightful loveliness] of the Lord...."

—Psalms 27:4 Amplified

Table of Contents

Acknowledgments

A friend of mine asserts that, in the interests of intellectual honesty, people surrounding a project of literary effort should be divided into two categories: "Thanks To…." and "No Thanks To…."

The first would include both encouragement and financial support, and other ways of saying, "We're for you; keep it up…." (if my grandmother were alive, she would have contributed in tangible ways like chocolate chip cookies). These are the ones Keith Miller calls your "balcony people"—the ones who cheer you on, the ones who lift you up, keep you going, who send you checks.

Then there are those Keith Miller calls your "basement people"—the ones who drag you down, discourage you, tell you, "It can't be done, no use trying, the odds are too great. Nobody in our family has ever done anything like it; you don't have the money, time, education, knowledge, contacts" etc. My friend, concerned about intellectual honesty, thinks these also should be listed. Of course, he's young, and idealistic/disillusioned—and probably right. Also, he assures me that no one ever reads *Introductions* and *Acknowledgements*.

The following are my "balcony people," the ones I owe a debt of persistent gratitude to for their encouragement, money, and chocolate chip cookies:

Kirby and Michelee Angell, Nikki Angell, Toby and Kim Angell, Dr. and Mrs. Warren M. Angell, Ray Blount, Barry and Janet Burks, James and Billye Coates, Vicki Coates, David and Susan Contreras, Ben and Donna Cranmore, Mike and Cyndi Curry, Ken and Brenda Hathaway, Steve and Phyllis Lindsey, Julie Angell Nadeau, Doyle and Janet Newman, Larry and Susan Pierce, Sherrill Poston, Gary and Joanna Scantlin, Jim and Rosa Scott, Dr. Kelly and Cindy Stephens, Dr. Tom and Annette Valley, Mike and Kerri Ward.

Since this is a Christian book, I'll have to forego the "*No Thanks To*" department—at least naming names. But you know who you are; shame on you.

"I can do all things through Christ who strengthens me."
—Philippians 4:13

Richard Angell

Introduction

I walked into my garage one day after almost thirty years of ministry, and saw rows of cardboard boxes containing sermon tapes from my first year onwards, yea, even unto the present day. My first thought: *Summer heat can't be good for audiotapes, especially after all these years.* My second thought: *There are at least that many boxes containing sermon notes languishing in closets, nooks and some crannies.* My third thought: *These tapes and notes represent my life's work, but few people listen to tapes anymore, unless they're driving or working around the house...*

After a millisecond of prayer, I decided to put them in written form for accessibility, posterity, and in the hopes that these messages would be of some help to others. I know my mother would like them. She was a big fan.

Someone has said that writing is easy; you just sit down in front of a typewriter/computer keyboard and open a vein. The process of preparing messages for services, seminars, radio broadcasts, articles, Bible studies, counseling, teen groups, etc., is much like opening a vein. I'm surprised there's a drip left.

In the course of time, my reading has, first of all, embraced the Bible; then C. S. Lewis, A.W. Tozer, Dietrich Bonhoeffer, Thomas Kelly, Thomas Merton, St. John of the Cross, R.C. Sproul, Jean-Pierre de Caussade, Brother Lawrence, Oswald Chambers, Keith Miller, Brennan Manning, Frederick Buechner, Francis Schaeffer, Anne Lamott, Jerry Bridges—and classic authors and poets, both Christian and throughout the literary world. I've also read a fair amount of history, science, anthropology, archeology, sociology, linguistics, psychology, religious doctrine of all faiths, and a great deal of what Charles Schulz had to say through Snoopy.

One recurring theme throughout my teaching and reading has been our idea of God. How we think of God is immensely important. Is he "Hairy Thunderer" or "Cosmic Muffin?" The pendulum swings to extremes from a harsh, impossible-to-please, hellfire-damnation entity to a permissive, casual, benign god—making no demands, giving no direction, caring little about transgressions. The truth, however, lies elsewhere. Jesus was always forcing inadequate ideas of himself (as God) to the surface of relationships: "Who are the people saying I am? Who do *you* think I am?"[1] "Why do you call me good? No one is good—except God alone."[2]

Do you want to know what God is *really* like? Jesus tells a story about a loving father who welcomes his prodigal son home with joy, forgiveness, restoration, and a celebration. Apparently, God does not require anything of us in order to return home, except the fact that we realize our life is not working out: "When he came to his senses, he said 'I will go back to my Father.'" (paraphrased)[3]

God as Father knows how difficult it is for us to love what is virtually an abstraction. So he gave us Jesus—God himself with a face, a personality, a human form, his divine love.

This collection of pieces gathered over a period of time explores the available, accessible, understanding, helpful, and friendly side of the vastness of God. God as an ocean, too large and incomprehensible to be fully known, can be experienced through the small portion—the inlet—that comes into our bay. If you read the quotes at the beginning of the book, you'll already be familiar with this idea.

Most biblical scholars believe the apostle John, exiled to the Isle of Patmos, lived much longer than the other martyred apostles. His mature wisdom never considers man and God apart from Jesus Christ. Christ is the near end of God—touchable, compassionate, strong, wise. He is the bridge, the one who fills the gap, the one who brings God close.

My writings are practical explorations of this reality; I'm glad they're not only deteriorating audiotapes in my garage anymore. My hope is they'll help you find the near end of God.

—RFA

Chapter 1

The Near End of God

Do you want to know what God is like? Let me tell you a story…

A man had two daughters. The youngest said to him, "Daddy, I don't want to go to college; I want to be on my own. Will you give me my college money so I can move away, get a job, and find out what life is all about?"

Against his better judgment, her father gave her the money and she moved to Los Angeles where she lived a life of parties, drinking, drugs, and sex. She was pregnant and broke; the man she was living with threw her out. She was desperate and had no place to go, then remembered, "My father's employees have jobs and benefits and I'm living on the street. Maybe my dad will at least give me a job."

She called her father and said, "Daddy, don't talk, just listen. I have really messed up my life. I don't expect you to take me back; I've wasted all you gave me. I'm pregnant and I have no place to go. I'm coming home on Friday; could you please just give me a job in the shipping department of your plant? I'll stay away from the house and I promise I won't embarrass you. If you're there to

19

meet the bus, I'll know I have a job; if you're not there, I'll just stay on the bus." Before her father could answer, she hung up the phone. On Friday, she returned home in fear and shame, not sure what she would have to face. As the bus pulled into the station, she saw her mother, but running to meet her was her father who embraced her, hugged her, kissed her.

She tried to say, "Oh Daddy, I've really messed up..." but her father wouldn't let her finish. By that time, her mother had caught up with them and her father said to his wife, "Let's get this kid to the house and get her cleaned up, then give her a good supper. Tomorrow you two can go shopping for her new clothes." Turning to his daughter, he said, "Let's call all your friends, tell them you're back, and have a big party. Baby, we all make mistakes. Your mom and I thought we might never see you again, and now here you are alive and back home, and we just have to rejoice and praise God for it!"[1]

Jesus told a similar story about a wasteful (prodigal) son. I have recast it as a wayward daughter in the hopes that the message would sneak up on you, that the significance would infiltrate your perception of God—because God is the father in the story. The story illustrates what God is like; instead of accusations and recriminations, the returning child is met with love, understanding, acceptance, and restoration. Our Heavenly Father is more interested in who we become in the future than in what we have done—or not done—in the past.

To return home to him, God doesn't require anything more than the realization that your life is not working out. Everything else comes later, when life can be handled from a position of strength in God's love. Failures and defeats are part of life; they can be used to gain understanding of others and ourselves.

One woman I know, in looking at the person she used to be, remarked, "I look at her, no longer with disgust and rejection, but with sympathy, compassion, and hope."

In Arthur Miller's play, *After the Fall,* the character Holga dreams that she gives birth to an idiot child. Even in the dream, she realizes the child represents her life. She is repelled; she wants to run away from it. Ultimately, she knows she must accept it, must kiss its grotesque face, must own the fact that her life is like an idiot child. "I think one must finally take one's life in one's arms…" she says.[2]

Blessed is he who frees us from self-loathing; then we can receive God's help for ourselves, identify with the struggles of others, and help them find what we have found: God that is touchable, accessible, warm, caring; the God who is near.

Harry Emerson Fosdick, one of the great preachers and writers, once wrote, "God can be thought of as Absolute Being; he is that. But in a crisis—where a man grapples with an unmanageable habit, or an abysmal grief—Absolute Being can be as distant, cold, and useless as the man in the moon. *What we need in a crisis is the near end of God:* God as we understand him, God as an available resource close at hand, our unseen friend, our invisible companion."[3]

Fosdick had never sailed the seas. In sermons he mentioned his summer cabin in Maine, and that he knew something about the ocean through the part that came near to him in the shores and inlets of his island. We know something of the vastness of God through the part we can touch—in ourselves, or in others.

Gert Behanna—a wealthy alcoholic, in and out of psychiatric sanitariums and divorced three times from wealthy men—was touched by the near end of God. She met her first Christians when in her mid-fifties—and quite drunk. She ridiculed them; they were kind to her. Finally the man said to her, "Gert, you are carrying a heavy load. Why don't you let God carry it for you?"

Gert said, "You make God sound like one of the redcaps at the train station, offering to carry my bags because they're too heavy."

"He looked me right in the eye and said, 'That's about the size of it.' He let me have God on the only terms I could take him…someone who wanted to carry my burdens…but if he had spouted theology, *or if he had quoted Scripture,* he'd have lost me, right there."[4] Gert became a wonderful, delightfully eccentric, down-to-earth Christian and a special communicator of God's grace. She helped many people find the near end of God.

We need a thorough grounding in the Scriptures; we need a growing knowledge of basic Christian doctrine. But when we are hurting—or helping hurting people—we need the Comforter, the Holy Spirit, often in human form. Like the little girl afraid of the dark, who was assured by her mother that God was with her, insisted, "But I need somebody with skin on." We need the reassurance of personal presence.

Christian writer Keith Miller tells a story from his own childhood that has touched many people, especially those who feel inadequate in times of others' grief and trauma. He was a young boy when his father died suddenly. The aftermath was lost in a daze for him, with people coming and going, bringing food and words of comfort, none of which he remembered. But one man he did remember—a tall rancher with face and hands Moroccan leathery from a lifetime of hard, outdoor work. The rancher sat quietly most of the evening, saying little to anyone. When he finally got up to leave, he shook Keith's hand and said, "I knew your daddy, son. He was a fine man." Then he left. Of all the visitors and guests, only this man stood out in Keith's memory. Not because of the words he said, but because he was there, a caring presence.

Often we shy away from hospital visits, tragic occasions, and funerals. We just "wouldn't know what to say." But sometimes just being lovingly *there* brings God near to hurting people. Words can be futile and hollow; love can fill a room with reassurance and hope for the future.

Thomas Merton once observed, "What is required of us now is not so much words, as to let people *feel* how Jesus lives in us."

One of the most touching funeral services I ever heard about involved the sudden death of a young child. The minister looked at the heartbroken parents and all those assembled there. Overcome by emotion, he stepped down from the pulpit, embraced the parents, and just cried with them. Afterwards, he dismissed the congregation. The people left without singing, without praying, without Scripture, without a sermon. But no one left without Jesus. No one left without feeling his love, his compassion.

Sometimes the near end of God is the person who unravels complex issues or complicated doctrine. During a break at a seminar, someone asked noted theologian Karl Barth if he could sum up his life's work in systematic theology in just a few words. Bystanders gasped at the effrontery of such a request of the great man. But Barth thought a moment, removed the pipe from his mouth, and said, "Yes, I think I can. It's this: Jesus loves me, this I know; for the Bible tells me so."[5] A simple, self-effacing summary. Maybe that's why he was a great man; he could bring the truth of God's Word near.

What have we been taught about God? What forms the basis of our conception of him? Is our picture of God formed from years of legalistic indoctrination, or from his own descriptions: the prodigal's father...the Good Shepherd...the one who protects us and guides us, the one who helps us become all we can be, the one who died for us?

Do you want to know what God is like? Let me tell you a story....

Chapter 2

. . . .

I Can't Do It

We're all really perfectionists at heart.

The *Optimist* says, "The glass is half full."

The *Pessimist* says, "The glass is half empty."

The *Perfectionist* says, "You've got twice as much glass there as you really need."

It's not only part of human nature to want things to be perfect; it's also part of God. Before the fall of man, we were in complete harmony with the divine nature and will. We have this "spiritual" genetic memory; we keep trying to get back to perfect.

This is why we keep "looking for love in all the wrong places."

Everyone—no matter how far away from God, no matter how twisted and perverted their desire—is looking for someone who really satisfies, completes them, and is perfect. Perfection means no more striving, no more leeches of desire screaming, "More, more!" It means nothing more needs to be added. Nothing more can be added. *It's finished.*

"It is finished."

Does that sound familiar?

It should. These were the words of Jesus on the Cross. The work of bringing mankind back to God has been accomplished. It's over. Nothing more *needs* to be done. Nothing more *can* be added. Perfection has been achieved.

But in everything else—our learning, our wisdom, our performance—perfection is a promise; it is yet to come. More specifically, we don't need to feel badly about many of the things we *do* feel badly about.

Trying to believe *is* believing. We may have concerns about the reality of our faith if we at times have doubts. Doubts can be the activity of the enemy; they can also be the natural operation of the mind's need to compare one possibility with another. The fact that we are concerned about our faith demonstrates that faith is already present.

We ask God to increase our faith; "Lord, help my unbelief." Though it may not be perfect faith, it is enough; use what you have. "If you have faith as small as a mustard seed, you can say to this mountain, 'Move...' and it will move."[1] God will add what is lacking.

Trying to pray *is* praying. All attempts at prayer, measured by perfect prayers, are less than perfect. We can pray for what we know about, but not for things we don't know. For this reason, the Holy Spirit is given, in part, to pray through us for the things we know not, with "those agonising longings which cannot find words."[2] Only the Holy Spirit prays perfectly. Pray as you can, not as you can't. When we pray, God will add the missing ingredients. We may have limitations; he does not. He knows all, sees everything, and reads our heart.

The slightest impulse towards prayer, any movement towards him, any inward monition of the most miniscule, God will see and honor. Prayer is movement towards God, however halting; not carefully arranged phrases.

Trying to love *is* loving. This is a critical area, because the missing ingredient in many relationships is *desire*. We may desire the other person or we may desire our own way, and still not desire the good of the other person. We can do what needs to be done with God's help, if we want to.

We don't do anything perfectly. Our sufficiency is not in ourselves, but in God. Never worry about having enough faith. God will honor whatever comes from your heart, not what you can do perfectly.

I can't do it. That's okay; God can. All I have to do is try.

Chapter 3

Misfits

Most of the progress in the history of the world has come from the action of misfits, malcontents, and rebellious individuals. Think about it for a moment; people who are content, settled, complacent, and well adjusted to their circumstances have little reason to initiate change. Those who are dissatisfied invent new ways of doing things, foment rebellion, and generally push the boundaries of civilization to new frontiers.

We don't usually think of the misfit as having anything but negative attributes, but the problem may be one of format. The willingness to risk, to live "outside the box," the restlessness, and the eternal "wanting something different"—in the right context—can become a powerful force that shapes events and alters destinies for the better.

Sometimes being a misfit isn't all that dramatic. Consider one of America's greatest resources—the immigrant. Not misfits in the usual sense, nevertheless, they don't "fit." Leaving behind the old country, the old ideas, the old ways, these seekers approach their life with new eyes. Old mind-sets have to change and be open to new possibilities. Innovation, creative combinations, risk of time and money—these things are needed to succeed. Immigrants become inventors, creators and start new businesses to carry out fresh ideas. Our country profits from their zeal, their inventive concepts, and their way of envisioning unforeseen benefits. America is the "land of opportunity" because life is not locked in and predetermined by a caste system or binding tradition; we are a nation of immigrants, founded by misfits.

If you've ever felt that you don't quite fit in, you're in good company.

In the Old Testament, the nucleus of David's mighty army was formed when "All those who were in distress or in debt or discontented gathered around him, and he became their leader."[1] The misfits of society became the foundation of David's kingdom. Their feats of bravery, exploits, and victories are recorded history; their descendants are today's Christians.

If you think that's too strong a statement, consider this: the apostle Paul reminds first century Christians that many of them were formerly thieves, drunkards, blackmailers, sexual deviates, and idol-worshippers.[2] This was their past, not their future; the energies that once resulted in evil were devoted to acts of courage. They were willing to risk more because they had less to lose.

God uses the cast-offs, the rejects, the failures, the misfits; they become warriors, heroes, and pioneers. God never looks at your past to determine your future. You may have known defeat and failure, but these are the conditions that clear the decks, create openness, make you aware of your need for God, and form the basis for future glory.

The information age is an unforgiving age. Our personal information can be stored within a database and is then available for analysis; unfavorable entries of the past can become, for all time, a part of that database and can restrict the future. Not so with God. The biblical record shows that he seeks the misfits of society for great purposes. Your past, no matter how ragged and chaotic, will never limit your standing with him or your opportunities in life when you put your life in God's hands.

A misfit, then, is usually a person who has not yet found his or her place. Here's another important point: that longing for something different is God's gift to you. If you haven't found your place, if you are restless, if you are incomplete, if you don't seem to fit anywhere, if you feel like an outcast, a reject, a malcontent, then you are open, searching, receptive, apt to be creative, and willing to risk something for fulfillment. Discontent is a gift that stirs you up, keeps you moving instead of stagnating.

History's greatest misfit was Jesus. The Scriptures tell us that he was *in* this world, but not *of* this world. He was a stranger, and rejection was the price; his home was not here. Unlike us, he knew his destiny. Jesus could fulfill his purpose by remembering he was a "sent one." Christ was on a mission; when it was finished he would return to his home. In the New Testament book of Philippians, the apostle Paul refers to the churches as "colonies of heaven." We are citizens of another kingdom; we are misfits here.

If you feel you don't belong, there may be a good reason for it. Let it make you a seeker. The attributes of the seeker are valuable; the promise to seekers is that they will invariably find what they are looking for.

That ought to make you feel better.

Chapter 4

. . . .

The Light
Must Be Gentle

We live in a world of broken hearts.

Some we know about, some we don't. To help others—
and ourselves—we must find a way to get past "the past,"
to bypass the failures that seal us off and make us unresponsive to
large aspects of life.

We help ourselves by helping others.

If we don't find a way through, a way to heal, then damaged
bodies and emotions, torn spirits, disappointments and ruined
dreams will result. "Scar tissue" becomes "scare tissue." We are
afraid to trust what reminds us of what has hurt so much before;
we avoid the people, events, and situations that echo that pain.

Most of us look good on the outside. Inside, many are curled
up in the fetal position with the electric blanket turned up to nine.
Defensive mechanisms are many and varied; walls of protection
are the most common.

The chick is hiding inside the egg.

Opportunities are limited behind the walls, inside the egg. It's
hard to be free, to be creative, to grow, to explore, to fulfill our-

selves in this known, warm, but confining place. Too big for the egg; too afraid to break out.

There are several ways to help free the chick from the confines of the egg.[1] In Christian circles, turning the heat up with hellfire preaching has moved a few chicks out. This method was popular in the past: *Cook 'em. Then they'll be afraid to remain stagnant; they won't dare to remain stagnant. Get them out and busy for the cause…*

There's another way to get chicks out of the egg—*Bash 'em. Once they've given their allegiance to Christ, brutal honesty will get them out of those shells. We'll tell them the truth about their shortcomings and failure.* This doesn't work very well, though. It turns the church into injustice collectors instead of encouragers, supporters, and ministers. The mentoring fads and "shepherding" movements have demonstrated this amply: *We'll crack their shells and get them out of there. The chicks may be a little damaged in the process, but we'll get them out.* Love was lost somewhere in the process.

Incubate 'em. This is best. The warm light of acceptance, friendship, and the simple telling of our own misadventures and learning process has a beautiful effect: the creation of a safe climate for confronting needs and opportunities, failures and fears. The little chick struggles towards the light, the warmth, and the acceptance; so do people. The effort is most successful if self-defense is not required. They may struggle, but they are stronger for it. These struggling ones can now bask in a nurturing, encouraging environment with examples of freedom all around them. Personal growth in the light of Christ's warm love now becomes paramount and, as we know from experience, is "more caught than taught."

A woman anointed Jesus with expensive perfume. Her sins, which were many, were drowned in his felt acceptance. Her need was expressed wordlessly. Only weeping was possible. Jesus was always easy on people, yet hard on what was hurting them. "A bruised reed he will not break, and a smoldering wick he will not snuff out."[2] She sensed his love and acceptance; there was no condemnation. He defended her from the verbal attacks of others; he cared about her and she felt it.

J.B. Phillips notes that "Just as he (Jesus) again and again brought down a theoretical problem to a personal issue, so we find here the Spirit of Jesus dealing not so much with problems as with people."[3] He healed wounded hearts and minds, often by his presence alone. In a saying attributed to St. Francis: "Go everywhere preaching the gospel (the Good News); if necessary, use words." People can sense the threat of judgment, the likelihood of accusations or disapproval; or they can sense the safety of common ground, of shared experience and respond to the candor of their own lives, their own mistakes.

Being open, transparent, and honest about our own need creates a climate of risk-free examination and growth for others. We are God's light-bringers. The love and acceptance we have in Christ shines a light through us that is warm and inviting. Like the chick, people instinctively move towards that light, and freedom.

Bernard of Clairvaux provided a masterful summation: "He who neither sees his sins nor confesses them is not illumined with light. But he for whom his sins loom so large that he despairs of forgiveness is drowned in light. Neither of these prays. What follows from this?

...The light must be gentle."[4]

Chapter 5

Grace Magnet

When my two sons were young—seven and nine, or thereabouts—they loved to swim. They had a hilarious, rambunctious time together; they were best friends. Swimming pools had on-duty lifeguards, but when streams and rivers were the "swimmin' hole," Dad was the lifeguard. This arrangement had a major drawback.

The drawback was that I was in my fly-fishing phase. I had beautiful split-bamboo fly rods, Orvis reels and all the tackle and equipment necessary to fool any fish. Watching that heavy line arc slowly out over the water, carrying that delicate, lightweight, beautifully-colored but deadly little fly on the end completely absorbed me. It landed softly, silently, and tenderly in pools and eddies along the bank where I hoped large, hungry fish were hiding. Rhythmic artistry...

It's mesmerizing. If you've seen the film *A River Runs Through It,* you have some idea of the beauty, power and poetry in the art of fly-fishing.

Since I was prone to distraction from my lifeguard duties, the rule was "If Dad is out of sight, put on your life jackets." This was not a popular edict because in those days, life jackets were large, round, pumpkin-like contraptions with complicated belts to hold them in place. The net effect was (1) you looked ridiculous; (2) the jackets were cumbersome and unwieldy on land and in the water; (3) your arms were held away from your body at an unnatural angle; and (4) obviously, you couldn't dive or swim underwater, which, for two small, energetic boys, was half the fun.

I had been drifting and dreaming, slowly wading and casting, watching the hypnotic line and tiny landing point of the fly in the water—then it hit me. I had been upstream and out of sight for over an hour. I had no idea if the kids were safe; no one else was around to help if they were in trouble. Fear, guilt, and panic ruled my mind. In a fast few seconds, I packed everything into a compact bundle and took the overland route, crashed through tangled, scratching brush and heavy undergrowth to get there *now* and wish it was sooner.

I still couldn't see the boys, but I could hear them. The splashing and laughter told me they were all right, and emotions eased. But when I pushed through the last few bushes and could see them, my heart melted. There they were, two little kids having as good a time as possible with their bulky life jackets on. They knew I was out of sight and faithfully followed the rule.

It would have been easy for them to say, "we forgot," or "didn't notice you were gone," or any of a dozen other excuses for doing what was fun rather than doing what was asked. They were the responsible ones that day. The aftermath, though, brought me into a surprising state: I felt such warmth and affection for them because of their willing compliance with a rule they didn't fully understand or agree with that, for some time afterwards, I couldn't do enough for them. Whatever they wanted, they got; I even suggested some fun things they hadn't yet thought of. I kept thinking of those two little guys wearing those despised life jackets, lovingly responding to my request.

I couldn't help reflecting *God must feel like this*. God is never irresponsible, like I can be; and certainly we are never out of his sight; but he is "our Father." Is there an action or a state of being that calls forth his generosity and abundance? Is there a "grace magnet?" Oh, yes.

I'm not suggesting God can be manipulated; I'm not impugning his sovereignty, or implying that he has to be bribed. The things he asks us to do—and not to do—are *for* us, in our best interest, for our benefit. He hates the things that hurt us and warns us against them. But no parent wants to be obeyed out of fear or duty. A real father wants a relationship through which his knowledge and practical wisdom can be imparted and received with love and respect.

When God sees our affectionate, faithful obedience, especially when we don't know all of the reasons behind what he asks, his lavish fatherhood is drawn out.

A doting grandfather was so generous to his two little grand-daughters during their weeks together at the lake that he was admonished not to spoil them by buying them everything in sight on the frequent trips into town. So he laid down a hard and fast rule: "I'll just buy them whatever they want and nothing more!" Love and generosity so great that restraint is called for! Is God really like this? Yes, and each of us could see all the good that follows from the slightest act of affectionate acquiescence on our part, if we were in the habit of counting our blessings.

A loving response on the part of his kids—that's us—to our heavenly Father is a grace magnet. The apostle Paul prayed that we would be able to "grasp how wide and long and high and deep is the love of Christ...who is able to do immeasurably more than all we ask or imagine...."[1]

Maybe that should be translated, "Let's just give the kids more than they can ask or imagine...and everything else." He has given us his Son; how could he now withhold anything?

Chapter 6

The Power of Forgiveness

That there is a power in forgiveness there can be no doubt. To be released through forgiveness, and walk on by one's own choice, independent of other's actions or attitudes, is to be free in the truest sense. It places the initiative for healing and wholeness in our own hands. God in his wisdom has not only required it of us but, as in so many things, has required it for our own benefit. And he has not placed our happiness and wholeness in the hands of others.

The power to forgive is a derived power, however. Only those who have truly received forgiveness can truly forgive others. If we have not received God's forgiveness, we can only enter into barter arrangements: "I'll forgive you *if* you'll admit your wrongdoing" but find it impossible and implausible to clear the slate without the other person's involvement. The injustice still rankles.

Consequently, when the Bible teaches that "if you do not forgive men their sins, your Father will not forgive your sins,"[1] it may be a statement of fact rather than a threat. Those who have truly known God's forgiveness cannot help but extend it to others. If it is difficult

41

for someone to forgive others, we begin to suspect that they have not yet been imprinted with God's love and forgiveness.

Demonstrations of this power can have great influence. At the proper time, our children must find God's forgiveness for themselves. What makes it easy for them is when we teach them forgiveness. Notice I didn't say teach them *about* forgiveness. Teaching about forgiveness is a matter of explanations, definitions, lectures. Teaching forgiveness is asking their forgiveness when we are wrong.

Many children have never had an adult ask their forgiveness. Worse, most have never heard an adult admit they were wrong. Yet all children know that adults are wrong from time to time. Adults get tired, depressed, upset, misunderstand; are pressured, hurried; they make mistakes and at times, they are unfair. Few things injure us more or make a more indelible impression than the injustice of some childhood events.

I can think of several in my own life: a broken promise by a teacher when I was in the third grade; unfair punishment resulting from a misunderstanding by a parent; times of being the innocent target of an adult's frustration and fatigue. I remember. So do you.

Do you want to *demonstrate* God's forgiveness to others? Or do you just want to *talk* about God's forgiveness?

If you want to teach your children God's forgiveness, ask their forgiveness.

When we ask our children to forgive us, it releases the power of forgiveness in them. The urging in them is to balance the scales, to follow suit, to reveal troubling events from the darkness of their past. Granting forgiveness gives them the power to ask forgiveness. Author Keith Miller provides the perfect example. While praying with his young daughter, he asks her forgiveness and God's for being unfair and harsh with her. When it's her turn to pray, she asks God to forgive her for "tee-teeing in the back yard last summer" instead of going into the house like she was supposed to. This minor infraction had weighed on her young mind all that time!

The power of demonstrated forgiveness creates a warm environment; the risk of rejection is lowered. We can come out of hiding, because we all have the same need. When we feel the shared nature of this journey, when we feel this nurturing climate, it is easier to be honest with ourselves and others—and God. More of our life is lived in God's healing light.

The healing power of demonstrated forgiveness not only benefits relationships, but is poured back into the physical, mental, emotional, and spiritual health of the one willing to forgive.

A family's supposed "run of bad luck" was under discussion; illnesses and accidents had occurred. Even more remarkable was the speed with which they were physically healed. One sour, illness-plagued woman remarked, "They aren't even particularly regular churchgoers, yet God seems to answer their prayers for healing almost immediately, while I cain't seem to git healed for love nor money."

Without passing judgment on her critical spirit, another remarked mildly, "On the other hand, a more forgiving family I've never known; they just don't seem to hold anything against anyone."

Those with spiritual experience know these are not coincidences. There is a power, both for others and for ourselves, when we demonstrate forgiveness. How many physical and mental illnesses could be traced to the slow corrosion of resentment and bitterness? Medical authorities differ as to the percentage, yet all agree the figure is quite high.

There is a graphic metaphor used in recovery literature: harboring hatred and unforgiveness towards someone is like drinking poison and then waiting for the other person to die. The effect is harmful and at times, deadly. The hurting people may realize the resulting harm in unforgiveness, but cannot bring themselves to finally forgive. Uppermost in their mind, the thing impossible to let go of, is how they have been hurt, how they have been wronged.

The power to forgive is derived from a firsthand conviction of the debt we owe—an enormous, unpayable debt God settled through his Son and has cleared the record. This debt no longer exists. Out of that massive sense of relief and release, if it has really occurred, we cannot help but clear the injustices, hurts, and wrongs done to us.

And we receive something important in return.

In an ancient story, a wealthy man—having nothing better to do after dinner—hauled an old trunk outside. The trunk was filled with promissory notes given to his family over many years. Most of them would never be paid, either because of deaths, moves, or inability to pay. He piled them up and set them on fire. As he sat back in his chair and watched the smoke rise lazily into the evening sky, he thought to himself, *Is this not power? Is this not freedom?*

Chapter 7

Fear Management

Turn base metals into gold? Sounds bizarre, doesn't it? It's called alchemy, and in medieval times those who practiced science and chemistry were chiefly involved in this pursuit. While the goal was never reached, in the attempt, other discoveries were made that greatly benefited mankind.

There is a "spiritual alchemy" that is very successful: man's unquestioned and impressive ability to turn a difficulty into a triumph, to change a minus to a plus, through the overcoming Spirit of Christ. And in the process, many other benefits and discoveries are realized.

In the Chinese language, the character for *crisis* is a combination of the symbols *danger* and *opportunity*. Assuming we can overcome the fear that often accompanies danger, we can usually find a way to turn potential defeat into an opportunity for victory. Jesus' first words to panicky people were "Fear not."[1] Fear management begins with the desire to find a turnaround solution; that alone focuses our attention on potential answers and away from fear-producing emotional states.

The keynote speaker at an important Washington, D.C. Conference on International Crisis Management gave a vivid demonstration of this principle. Delegates from many countries were present. He was introduced and making his way to the platform when his nose unaccountably began to bleed. Holding his handkerchief to his nose helped, but the spreading bloodstain made the problem more visible and dramatic to his audience.

In public settings like this, onlookers feel a great deal of fear vicariously: *What if that were me? What will he do? What can he do?* The tension is palpable and raises everyone's fear to new levels. The audience feels sorry for the speaker, identifies with his predicament, while feeling both confused and panicky. Time to turn a minus into a plus—but how?

The speaker was equal to the challenge. After mentally asking God for the solution, or at least the next step, God's answer came. Still holding his bloodstained handkerchief to his nose, he calmly looked out over the assembled conference for a long minute, waited while the suspense grew to maximum pitch, then said, "Where but in Washington D.C. can you hear an address on crisis management and watch a man bleed to death at the same time?" The applause was deafening. He received a standing ovation twice: once immediately, and again at the end of the speech.

He didn't bleed to death; neither did he die from embarrassment or fumble his big moment. He delivered a memorable address with a bloodstained handkerchief at his nose. The release of tension came in the form of thunderous applause and a standing tribute for two reasons: he gave a living demonstration of his topic, crisis management. More importantly, he was applauded for his indomitable spirit. Because people present identified with him in his predicament, each felt his success was their own. Everyone felt like celebrating and they did. They felt good about themselves, and he was the hero who brought it about. Needless to say, he felt fantastic!

Our happiness does not lie in fleeting pleasures, but in overcoming obstacles. We are all tempted to quit at times, but we should never quit as losers. We can train ourselves to persevere until we find a way to turn a minus into a plus; after we have mastered the situation, then we can quit or move on. It is remarkable how often our so-called reasons for quitting were nothing more than the desire for an easy life free of taxing difficulties. If we give in, our internal appraisal of ourselves is bound to suffer and we will never know the happiness from conquering a really tough problem.

Unexpected benefits will accompany each attempt to turn a minus into a plus. A young bride found herself often alone in a small house close to the Mojave Desert, her army husband away on maneuvers and training exercises much of the time. She wrote her parents in despair, complaining of unbearable heat—125 degrees in the shade of a cactus with nothing but prairie dogs, snakes, and sand. Her father wrote back, quoting a few lines from a poem, "Two men looked out from prison bars. One saw mud, the other saw the stars."

She began to try to see the stars and found a wondrous world of mystery and beauty that is the desert. Looking closely, she saw many small life forms, and fascinating plants and animals. She became so knowledgeable about her surroundings, so imbued with the desert's vast majesty and greatness, that she wrote a best seller using the desert as a setting. *Bright Ramparts* by Thelma Thompson is still available today.[2]

Thelma Thompson used a little spiritual alchemy and turned a minus into a plus.

So did a Florida man, who inherited a "useless" parcel of land supporting nothing but scrub trees and rattlesnakes. Lots of rattlesnakes. Big rattlesnakes. Huge rattlesnakes. With his own brand of spiritual alchemy, he transformed that barren place into a tourist mecca: the world's largest rattlesnake farm exporting canned rattlesnake meat; skins for boots, shoes, purses, belts, wallets, luggage, and other products; poison extracted for laboratory production of anti-venom toxin; exhibits and displays in a town renamed Rattlesnake, Florida, that plays host to thousands of tourists each year. Spiritual alchemy made him a multi-millionaire.[3]

This is a spiritual process. One man goes down in defeat; another comes along, takes up the same challenge and succeeds. What makes the difference is the God-given ability, when believed in and acted upon, to find the seeds of creative opportunity in miserable, difficult, and sometimes life-threatening situations. It begins with the desire to change a minus into a plus, and several things happen: fear and despair are bypassed in the search for a solution. The outlook now becomes outward and positive, not inward and negative. With an open, expectant viewpoint, ideas, resources, and divine revelations become visible that were blocked by fear-choked perceptions and emotions. Like the one who fashioned us, we become resourceful, creative beings, receiving whatever is needed to handle any situation.

By experience, we come to know that God is *for* us. To believe that God doesn't want us to succeed is to believe that God doesn't care if we fail. Everything in the Bible refutes this idea; one of the key Scriptures is Jeremiah 29:11: "'For I know the plans I have for you,' declares the Lord, 'plans to prosper you and not to harm you, plans to give you hope and a future.'"[4]

"If God is for us, who can be against us?"[5] is the apostle Paul's great challenge to our defeatist tendencies. Infused with the unstoppable Spirit of Christ, we can overcome. The cross is the most powerful symbol of victory in all of recorded history over the greatest enemy, death. It is the biggest plus sign known to man, and a constant reminder of God's ability to turn an enormous minus into an incredible plus.

In his name, he will help us do the same.

Chapter 8

Pray as You Can, Not as You Can't

Maybe this is all just a product of your overly-active imagination....

This was an all too familiar voice. I came to know Christ in 1976. Owning my own business meant there was plenty to pray about. In that first year, I would often hear the voice of the adversary: *How do you know you really belong to God? Maybe you're just imagining all this; maybe you're just fooling yourself...*

Then the doubts began to flood in. A particularly vivid scene comes to mind: I was walking out the back door of my office building, into the parking lot. The thought that I should just forget all about being a Christian came forcefully upon me. *Maybe the answer to life's problems was in a different philosophy, or way of life...*

But I need someone I can talk to.

I began to pray using simple, everyday words, and the confusion of the attack melted away. I was not alone; God was with me.

God does not want us to lead anxious, fretful lives; he wants us to recognize the attacks of the enemy, to know he will take care of us. "Do not be anxious about *anything*, but in everything, by prayer and petition, with thanksgiving, present your requests to

God. And the peace of God, which transcends all understanding, will guard your hearts and your minds in Christ Jesus."[1]

The key to the fulfilled and confident life is obviously prayer. But prayer can be an area of defeat for those who have been taught impossibly high standards, criteria for the amount of time that "must" be spent, or repetitive rituals that make prayer tiresome and unattractive.

One of the best principles for overcoming difficulties is to "pray as you can, not as you can't;"[2] to pray in a way that brings a real sense of connection to your time with the Lord, even if it doesn't fit someone else's format.

I once knew a very godly man; his presence was a benediction you could literally feel. The source of his sanctity, however, was not his many degrees and honors, or his scholastic achievements; it was his simple, unassuming, yet uniquely meaningful time in prayer.

Every morning he had a cup of coffee with God.

He would rise early, brew two cups of coffee (he says with a smile, "God takes his black, but I like a little cream and sugar in mine"), and sit at the kitchen table and talk over his upcoming day, visualizing Jesus in the chair opposite him. Reading a Scripture, asking counsel of his friend, listening and making his requests known, drinking coffee in the peaceful early morning with all the attendant aromas…no wonder his spiritual life shone through so clearly. His time with the Lord made Jesus real to him.

For many years, my favorite method for making Jesus real to me has been inspired by the visual images of the old hymn "In the Garden," especially the line, "And he walks with me, and he talks with me, and he tells me I am his own." We do just that. I am in modern clothes, Jesus is in his traditional white robes; we walk in the early morning garden setting of the hymn, "while the dew is still on the roses."[3]

He listens to me: I listen to him. We talk things over. Jesus is personal to me. That's the point of prayer; to pray as you *can*, to feel that he is real, to know that he cares.

Another friend of mine accomplishes this in his own special way. He stops at the 7-11 store on the way to his construction job to get a cup of coffee and spend a few moments with God (it may not be possible to be a real Christian without drinking coffee!). He parks his car at the side of the store's parking area, reads a passage of Scripture, lets it sink into his heart as he meditates on it, then seeks God's guidance and help through his workday and home time. His family gets up at the proverbial crack of dawn—and noisily; by leaving a few minutes early for work, he can spend time alone with his Lord.

"What's a poor mother to do with a house full of quarrelsome, headstrong children?" Madalene Harris bemoans her predicament in a wonderful chapter in the book *How To Improve Your Prayer Life*. In the chapter entitled "Bearing One Another's Burdens," she tells the story of a unique and adventurous approach to prayer, made necessary by her husband's long absences and her relative isolation in a beautiful but remote mountain setting.

> "I tried to postpone major decisions and severe disciplinary action until my husband returned. But problems merely intensified, and I soon discovered two indisputable facts: neither discipline nor decisions can be delayed where young children are concerned, and settling disputes was the last thing my husband welcomed during his few days home."

She talks about her time with the Lord. When the children left for school, she would take her Phillips New Testament and her well-worn devotional book, *Streams In the Desert*, jog a mile or so along a nearby stream, find a secluded spot, and pour out her heart to the Lord.

> "Amazing things happened. Attitudes changed; the noise level at our house decreased; my nerves grew steadier. I discovered that the children's temperaments (and my own) improved in direct proportion to my faithful prayer vigil on their behalf."

She continued her prayer adventures by applying her prayer approach to the needs of others, writing names on a sheet of paper kept in her Bible, as the Lord seemed to direct her.

"My prayer life, which had begun out of desperation, was being swept along by the spontaneous winds of daily anticipation of God at work." [4]

Writing down prayers—not only names of those we intercede for—is an ancient and important method of deep communication with the Lord. Many of the psalms were intense, urgent prayers written down; we have them today because someone poured out their heart on a writing surface. We know the benefit of this prayer method; nothing goes deeper and makes a more permanent imprint than a thought we can study and re-read as we pray.

But I am a private person. My thoughts, particularly my honest prayerful thoughts, are very revealing. I hesitate to express myself candidly and fully in a prayer journal for fear it might be discovered and read by someone else. Journals are a valuable and effective tool for some, but I don't want to run the risk of intrusion into personal areas. As someone said, "If my thoughts were projected onto a screen in the public square, I'd have to leave town."

My solution is to honestly and clearly write down my prayer, meditate, ask God for insight and direction, and then make a little ritual out of burning them to ashes—a private burnt offering unto the Lord.

Brother Lawrence's program of "practicing the presence of God" is a way to "pray without ceasing."[5] He would try to remain as much as possible with God in his thoughts, no matter what the daily activity. "He believed it was a serious mistake to think of our prayer time as being different from any other. Our actions should unite us with God when we are involved with our daily activities, just as our prayer unites us with him in our quiet time."[6]

Powerful prayers can be just a few, deeply felt emotions expressed in broken, poignant phrases. A touching example occurs in the film *Romero,* when the Archbishop, played by Raul Julia, prays the ultimate prayer of surrender and consecration: "I can't...you must...I'm yours...."[7]

It's better to pray as we can—and *pray*—than to forsake regular prayer because we can't do it perfectly. *Trying* to pray *is* praying. We don't do anything perfectly. In this matter of prayer, as in all things, we need God's help. He makes it perfect.

Chapter 9

Wasteful Love

Why this waste? This perfume could have been sold at a high price and the money given to the poor!"

The scene is a supper at the home of Simon the Leper (imagine being burdened with that name down through the ages!). As the guests reclined at table, a woman arrives, breaks open an alabaster jar of very expensive ointment and anoints Jesus' head. She is greatly criticized by angry onlookers.[1] But Jesus comes to her defense: "She has done this for me...to prepare me for burial. What she has done will always be told as a tribute to her."

True love, by its very nature, is excessive; if it is real, it is bound to be lavish, extravagant, flamboyant and spontaneous. Love is not subject to the usual logical processes of practical evaluation. It is not calculated, measured or carefully controlled. Real devotion to someone blinds us to selfish considerations; it is not how little I can get away with giving, but how much I can give. The story of the widow's mite teaches us that it is not the amount given, but how much of ourselves, or all of our resources, that we give.

Another aspect of real love is that it lives in the moment—this moment. Not only is it extravagant in its expression, but it is impulsive. It must give full expression now, because this moment will never come again. The next moment requires the next expression. Love must act now so that the beloved will experience its reality now.

Love is an action verb. A spiritual teacher was once asked for his definition of love. He told the questioner that he would not like the definition. When asked why, the teacher replied, "Because it has nothing to do with emotion apart from action; love is something you do."

What people really *mean* is expressed in what they *do*. If someone tells you they love you but mistreats you, demeans you or abuses you, then you should instinctively know that what is said is not what is meant. Many people, especially young people, are often confused by the mixed messages of abusive people and come to equate "love" with pain. No wonder so many vulnerable people become distrustful and insulated, inoculated against real relationship.

In the Bible, the highest value, surprisingly, is not truth but love. The apostle Paul wrote the entire thirteenth chapter of 1 Corinthians to make the point that you can be *truthful* and still harsh, hurtful and unloving; even great sacrifices are worthless unless they begin in love. No philosophy, regardless of its nobility or power to persuade, can be regarded as truth unless it results in greater love as defined in the Bible. Truth is subservient to love; therefore, we need a standard based on love. If situations confuse and rules conflict—even if others misunderstand our actions and decisions—we will always be right in God's eyes if we do the loving thing.

The sweet expression of adoration and devotion from a prostitute, who lavished a beautiful fragrance upon her Lord, remains as a lasting legacy of love. Jesus even commented, "Her sins, which are many, are wiped away because she loved much."

True love is wasteful. The lover ignores boundary lines and limitations. Laws, rules, regulations—all are finite; true love goes on forever.

Even death cannot stop it.

Chapter 10

Carefully Careless

Oswald Chambers, one of the shining spiritual lights of the past, is responsible for the best-selling devotional book of all time.

Sharing the hope of Christ with U.S. soldiers in the North Africa ministry tents of the YMCA during the First World War, Chambers never thought of someday being a best-selling author.

That's because he never wrote a book. His messages were taken down in shorthand by his wife, Biddy, and later, after his death, compiled into a series of books bearing his name. The best known is the classic devotional book, *My Utmost for His Highest*.

In desperate circumstances, he once said to Biddy, "Let us keep very near Him and wait."[1]

This could be a valuable strategy for God's people today. Activity, arranging, planning, preparation—these have the *semblance* of progress; praying and waiting for God's certainty would be a more advantageous position. Taking swift and decisive action is often a way of avoiding prayer and trust, a way to take matters into our own hands. Immediate resolution results; the die is cast; just ask God to bless it.

But the future still lurches forebodingly toward us. The French philosopher Montaigne said, "My life has been filled with terrible misfortune, most of which never happened."

Worry usually centers on things that loom as potential disasters in the future; rarely do they center in the things of the moment. We can handle those, deal with and make provision for things present. To experience loss is often not as bad as to contemplate loss. Socrates expressed it this way: "Often, it is much easier to lose your garden than to go to court and fight for it." And much of what we fear never happens, arousing energy and anxiety for nothing.

This statement by Oswald Chambers describes the core of the problem: "The one great crime on the part of a disciple, according to Jesus Christ, is worry. Whenever we begin to calculate without God we commit sin."[2] Worry is the contemplation of possible futures, using only our meager and inadequate resources as a measuring rod of likely success. Worry projects an outcome without God's income, without God's input, without his plan and contribution. Worry leaves out God's motives and stated purpose: "'For I know the plans I have for you,' declares the Lord, 'plans to prosper you and not to harm you, plans to give you a hope and a future.'"[3]

Chambers' advice to those facing uncertainty was, "Trust God and do the next thing."[4] Waiting does not always mean inactivity; at times, it means the faithful fulfillment of known duties, the meeting of daily responsibilities in the spirit of confidence and contentment.

Author and Bible teacher Jerry Bridges' classic comment puts it succinctly: "Contentment is believing that God is good to me right now." Right now, regardless of the circumstances, I am content in God's plan (even if I don't know the fullest extent of that plan) and God's motive (I always know the fullest extent of his motive: his love for me and desire to give me a "hope and a future").

One of the great modern day spiritual encouragers was Gert Behanna. She was a rough-talking recovering alcoholic, married and divorced three times to prominent, wealthy men. In a taped testimony, she told of meeting Christ late in life, buying a large house to provide a safe harbor for girls in trouble, and then giving away the rest of her considerable wealth.

Her spiritual formula for relying on God's guidance and avoiding anxiety was this: "Is this for God, or is this for Gert? If it's for God, we try to do it; if it's for Gert, we try not to do it. If we don't know, we wait."[5]

Gert's statement gives us three simple, usable directions for a peaceful, productive life:

- Willing, loving submission to God's known will. Gert's expression is charming: "If it's for God, we try to do it." We acknowledge that we may not be able to do it perfectly, but we try.
- Resist what God doesn't seem to want. We refuse to act against his known will. We don't even do that perfectly; we *try* not to do it.

Then the most beautiful part of all:

- If we don't know, we wait. This is ultimate peace. We rest in the knowledge that God's will is *exactly* what we would desire if we knew everything that God knows. His plan embraces potential and fulfillment. God's "no" or his silence is never his final answer; sometimes he just asks us to wait.

He is the way-shower, the guide. It is God's responsibility to make his will clear, his responsibility to make his way plain. This is not speaking disrespectfully; it is acting decisively, submitting to God in a state of obedience. We pay God a great compliment to delay action until we are reasonably certain of his direction. And the peace that follows Gert's simple plan is "the peace that transcends all understanding."[6]

The plan embraces obedience, resistance to temptation, and watchful waiting, including a simple reliance upon God to help us do even the smallest things. We include him in all we do, hold a state of total readiness to do his will, and remember that we need him for everything.

We can then be "carefully careless."

Early in my preaching ministry, I taught "carefully careless" to a group of spirited young Christians, who took my teaching to heart and expressed it by saying, "I have this problem, such and such is threatening or happening, but *I don't care.*" The statement was not meant to be flip, nor did it mean their head was in the sand and they were ignoring the challenge. It was a simple and concise way to communicate their stance: they personally did not have to take care of the problem. The care had been transferred to Another, and they were carefully care-less.

Instant peace.

They were honoring God by standing ready to follow his guidance, equally ready to stop when he indicated. In the meantime, worry was absent. When asked about their current situation, the problem was truthfully stated, but the burden was not assumed. Others in the group understood, would pray effectively, and know their state of mind was clear and worry-free.

Deeply spiritual men and women believe that Satan's favorite strategy is to urge people to act, to make decisions, to move without taking time to pray. This is particularly true of the adversary's work in the modern world, where fast-moving events seem to glorify instant, on-the-spot decisions. For example, in the business world, your management skills—your right to lead—are often linked to the perception that you can make lightening-fast decisions, giving orders with authority as if from vast available wisdom.

After all, that's how it's done when life is fired at you point-blank: the adrenaline rush kicks you into a higher gear, and underlings say, "Wow!" and aspire to have your job (this may not be a good thing, for this reason alone!). They want to feel that energy; they want to make big salaries and look important. Satan takes advantage of the momentum of life to keep us from thinking, to keep us from praying.

God will always give you time to consult him. The voice that urges us to *Do it now, you'll lose out if you don't take advantage of this wonderful opportunity, only available to those who can take action, invest now, do it, act! Act!* is always the voice of the enemy.

Whenever we begin to calculate without God, we commit sin. This thought of Chambers' resonates in our deepest part. Here is a rule of life, especially in making decisions: God will always give us time to pray. Always. Period.

Why would there be any exception to this rule? We are his sheep, and he is our Shepherd. We know his voice and another we will not follow—if we take time to hear the voice. It honors him that we want to hear him, and that we won't move until we're sure. We will surely miss out on some "great" opportunities—Satan's opportunities. In today's pragmatic, results-oriented society, what's *good* is what *works*. Satan's suggestions may work and be successful in every respect. But even if Satan's ideas prove to be profitable or even harmless later, they are not the ones God wants us to have.

In a televised political debate, a candidate was asked if he would have made the same decision his opponent had recently made. His answer was a secular classic: "It depends on how it comes out." But candidates cannot know the future; this cannot be the basis for a decision. This is outcome-based wishful thinking, not the application of principle; certainly not a biblically-based platform for decisions. The proof of something's rightness for us is not whether it works out or is successful, but rather if God originates it; then he will work it out. If he does, it will be for our benefit. Otherwise, even the best things can be a curse. The Bible teaches, "The blessing of the Lord brings wealth, and he adds no trouble to it."[7] This same verse in the King James Version promises, "He adds no sorrow to it."

The test is… is it of God?

If it's for God, we try to do it. If it's for us, we try not to do it. If we don't know, we wait.

Waiting can be a time of confident, contented activity, with the future held in trust, even in the direst circumstances. Relaxed confidence is the mark of the spiritual master, and pays the ultimate compliment to God. "Even though I walk through the valley of the shadow of death, I will fear no evil, for you are with me; your rod and your staff, they comfort me."[8]

These intimate ones walk close to God, and can even laugh and make jokes at times that seem almost incongruous. They are light of heart in the heaviest of moments. "The Lord is my shepherd, I shall not be in want..."[9]

"Chambers possessed a rare capacity to trust matters to God in prayer and wait for Him to move,"[10] reports David McCasland in his biography *Oswald Chambers: Abandoned To God*. "There was no discrepancy between Oswald's walk with God and his talk, and in the final analysis, that was the power of his influence."[11]

"Sticking resolutely to his unspoken motto in every circumstance, 'I refuse to worry.' Without anxiety, he welcomed each day and its developments under the sovereign hand of God."[12] "Let God engineer."[13]

This has ever been true of the saints of the Lord: an almost perfect match-up between the inner and outer person, a total reliance on God evidenced by their lack of concern for what might be. "Future plans are uncertain, but we all know that there is first God's plan to be lived, and we can safely leave everything to Him, 'carefully careless' of it all."[14]

No one has said it better.

Chapter 11

The Mystery of the Wounded Healer

He saved others; himself he cannot save."[1]
These mocking words directed at the suffering Savior on the cross echo a mystery found throughout the Bible. We know Jesus could have saved himself, but only in his refusal to do so was our intimacy with God possible. Jesus did not offer a system or an organization; he did not offer a plan or an ideology. He offered himself; he suffered on purpose. In his wounds we find the reality of our healing; in his brokenness, a releasing of resurrection power.

The source of healing is sacrifice. All true healers find the wellspring of their curative power in an outer or inner wound. Wounded healers offer the simple, accessible concern of God; no complicated doctrines, just the knowledge of a common ground of pain and suffering rising from the shared nature of their human journey.

It takes one to help one. There is nothing like a recovering alcoholic to really help another alcoholic. The wounded healer may not have the same affliction, but has undoubtedly experienced the same fears, hurts and doubts.

Without this empathetic common ground, the healer's attempt to help comes off as well-meaning advice from a person strong enough or smart enough to avoid pain; an indefinable sense of superiority that suggests, *If you were just more like me, these things wouldn't be a problem.* Consider the parable Jesus told about the log and the speck. He is not advising us to refrain from helping people; rather, he is teaching us that as we deal with life's larger issues, then we will see clearly to help others with small areas of their need.

Out of the worst part of your life—the most shameful and destructive—will come the best part of your life, fulfilling the God-given destiny of helping to heal others. Nothing need ever be lost. These areas of lack draw God to us, not the things we have done perfectly, or at least very well. None of us are black sheep; we are all "love sheep." He is drawn to us because of our need, and he uses what we have in common with all mankind to help others.

Whether we know it or not, we are all wounded healers. We may not be able to point to massive trauma or tragic circumstances; our wounds run much deeper than what may be visible or knowable to others. The wounds exist, are intrinsic to us as human beings, and assert their influence. Our wounds—and therefore, our weaknesses—reveal themselves in our insecurities, defensiveness, selfishness, and our vigorous defense of our moral certainty. But, you have to know you're wounded; you have to know you have a need only God can fulfill. In the turning to him, the power to heal others is in some way released.

The specific ways that we turn to him, apart from simple acknowledgement, all contain the essential element of sacrifice:

- Prayer. We not only pray for what hurts us, we pray for who hurt us. In the book, *Finding God at Harvard: Spiritual Journeys of Thinking Christians,*[2] Psychiatrist Robert Coles interviews Ruby Bridges, a young black child who ran a gauntlet twice a day through a screaming, jeering white mob just to attend school. She told Coles she was praying for the hecklers: "If you're going through what they're doing to you, you're the one who should be praying for them." Ruby said she learned this from her minister at church. Through this means of sacrifice, our own hurts begin to dissolve.

- Fasting. Unparalleled as an act of sacrifice. Jesus spoke as if fasting would be a periodic, expected practice, especially in difficult circumstances. "This kind (of demonic entity) comes out only by prayer and fasting."[3] Even when circumstances are not desperate, fasting hones our spiritual receptivity, and demonstrates a serious willingness to receive God's direction.
- Watchfulness. A state past verbal prayer, a state of waiting; a condition of interior silence, without thought of specific gain or answer. The watchfulness called for in the Scriptures is not a passive state of negation, but an active state of prayer using the whole being, the whole body, our whole history, our whole experience.

"Making one's own wounds a source of healing, therefore, does not call for a sharing of superficial personal pains but for a constant willingness to see one's own pain and suffering as rising from the depth of the human condition which all men share."[4]
—Henri Nouwen

Chapter 12

Holy Motivation

Much of the time, our decisions are made on the basis of what we hope to see happen. We try to project the end result and act accordingly. This is a valid principle for most of life, but has limitations in some of the biggest and farthest-reaching actions we take—especially when it involves our spiritual priorities.

We know the principles of God's Word (or should), but do not always know where they will take us.

Abraham is the shining example; he responded to God's call without knowing where the journey would take him: "Abraham believed God, and it was credited to him as righteousness."[1] He trusted in a *person*, not a fully-revealed plan. Abraham was a trusting, hopeful, man of faith; he believed God could do the impossible. He was adventurous; security was a secondary issue. Because of these qualities, he became the "father of our faith."

Everyone in the Old Testament symbolizes aspects of God's message to us. We will find times when God's message and character will be far more known to us than the future or any certainty.

Knowing and being fully convinced of the love God has for us will help us trust him: "And so we know and rely on the love God has for us."[2] God's "tenacious tenderness"[3] is depicted in the Scriptures through the parables and teachings of Jesus, in passages such as the Good Shepherd and the Prodigal Son.

To trust our heavenly Father, we need to know he takes the long view; his purposes will be worked out in our lives over time. He will also make use of our failures and apparent defeats, as well as our victories, and encourage us to grow by using setbacks as faith strengtheners. One of the big lessons we learn is perseverance, a quality developed by applying steadfastness consistently.

C.S. Lewis said, "We are not necessarily doubting that God will do the best for us; we are wondering how painful the best will turn out to be."[4] With God, however, the discomfort will have a purpose; life has pain no matter what, often meaningless apart from God.

Dietrich Bonhoeffer, the German pastor who chose to return to Germany and endure the Nazi regime with his people, felt that he could not lead them *after* the war if he did not share the risks with them *during* the war. His biographer notes, "What he had chosen was by no means clear. *His reasons for choosing were far clearer than what he had chosen!*"[5]

We are results-oriented people. Trusting is not in our nature until we adopt God's view of life; this is a different perspective to us. We like success but there are higher values. Here is one of them: "It is better to fail in a cause that will ultimately succeed than to succeed in a cause that will ultimately fail."[6]

We don't plan to fail; but success and failure can't always be measured the world's way. Act on principle, not on projected results—the principle of trusting God and his Word. This is what success is for a Christian.

Chapter 13

Spaces

I t's not the blanket on top of you that keeps you warm; it's the part that hangs over the edge. It's the frame and the mat that highlights the painting, drawing the eye in, that makes the painting look important. It's the pauses that make the preaching powerful. From the quiet times we draw the wisdom and strength to persevere and overcome.

"At daybreak Jesus went out to a solitary place."[1] Withdrawing to a desert or deserted place was characteristic of Jesus' spiritual life. He knew his time was limited, and the needs of the people were great, but still Jesus took time to be in the Father's presence, to be alone, to pray, and meditate. Then he moved into public places for teaching and miraculous works of power. From the times apart—the spaces in his life—came the thrust of knowledge and action.

What makes a sanctuary holy is not bricks, mortar, glass and steel. What makes a sanctuary holy is a living Presence, the moving of the Spirit of God. "The spirit can move only into open spaces that await filling, into a longing that awaits satisfaction. Without silence, there can be no music. Without empty spaces, we have no room to be filled with good things. Our task is to live with wide margins, amply surrounded by empty places and silent spaces."[2]

Reserve power and divine resources inevitably emerge from those quiet times in our lives, even if we are not aware of them at the time we receive them. When the moment comes, when the need is there, the right word, the right thought, the right action is activated, just as in Jesus' life.

Our lives are driven by many activities fueled by guilt. Complexity and duty conspire to force a frenzied attempt to be all and do all. Keeping wide margins in our lives is difficult; time for ourselves must be valued, instituted, and defended.

Here are some thoughts on first steps towards voluntary simplicity, toward making spaces in our daily lives:

- Avoid being drawn into over-commitment through guilt. This is a common trap for parents. By implication and pressure, parents feel they must attend every game, dance, hobby, and activity of (usually) a multitude of kids; otherwise, you're a "bad" mommy or daddy.

- Eliminate clutter. That garage, closet, car, or living/dining/bedroom full of junk is a mental weight and brings psychological overload. The spaces must exist in your visual format as well as in your time.

- Value quiet and rest. These qualities must first be a priority in order for them to exist at all. Too much will compete and crowd quietness out in the "tyranny of the urgent." This is the category of prayer, but is not limited to prayer. Time for reflection on the past, present, and future blessings was the original idea of Sunday, a day of rest.

- Cultivate the timeless. Thoreau's famous statement "Read not the Times. Read the Eternities"[3] will help direct us to reading, music, and thinking that gives us a sense of what lasts, the permanent, the indestructible. A part of this step is seeking that which represents quality in all pursuits; certainly what passes for most entertainment will fail this test.

- Don't overbuy. An abundance of discretionary income can result in overspending. Families tend to purchase back-up items or clothing to ensure security of ownership, or just for convenience. Owning less means less to insure, less to keep track of.
- Cultivate family traditions. Predictable, dependable rituals have staying power in our lives. Memories, quality of life, and the sense of belonging help bond us to each other. These spaces are priceless, and children especially use them to create an identity unshakable in later years.

Shared difficulties can also knit people together. Famed writer and teacher Leo Buscaglia tells a memorable story about his father who was frequently out of work in their very poor country. He would call everyone in the family together—aunts, uncles, and all the children—to give out assignments. Everyone had a job to bring in money, even the little kids. His father would tell them, "We've all got to pull together to make sure this family makes it." Leo said he never, in his entire life, felt so secure, so much a part of something important, so needed, as when his father would remind them that "we've all got to pull together to make sure this family makes it."

- For health, long life, and peace of mind, cultivate a strong faith. Daily devotionals, memorizing passages of God's Word, being part of a church family, and doing our part in a church family, all help create notable traditions, strong ties, and the knowledge of God's goodness.

Spaces are important to us. Through them, God's "still, small voice" of reassurance, provision, guidance, protection, and peace can always be heard. We need his voice now more than ever.

Chapter 14

¿Para Hoy?

P ara Hoy?"
"*For today?*" The question came from a woman selling fruit in a Latin American, open-air marketplace, and it was a good question: "Do you want it for today, or will you keep it for a while?"

The answer was important and impressive:

"*Si. No tengo vida fuera de hoy.*" (Yes. I have no life beyond today).

While this may be a particularly Latin American perspective on life, it holds a great truth if we are to live without anxiety and uncertainty. God's provision through manna was only for one day. The ripe fruit of this day is *now*.

We must make plans for the future—take out insurance to manage risk; plan for the expected and unexpected. But the Bible teaches specifically that the only way to happiness is to place our trust in God for each day as it comes our way.

Many of the Twelve Step programs are based on this principle: you don't have to give up drinking or drugs forever. You only have to commit to giving it up "one day at a time." The principle is a sound biblical formula for peace of mind. I don't have to make a decision, right now, for the rest of my life; I only have to make a decision that commits me to a particular way of life for the next twenty-four hours.

Jesus emphasized this truth: "Therefore do not worry about tomorrow, for tomorrow will worry about itself. Each day has enough trouble of its own."[1]

This was a folk saying in Jesus' day. He quoted it to reaffirm its truth: the initial level of understanding is "don't borrow trouble." The underlying meaning is the old time-honored refrain, "Live one day at a time." The thing may or may not happen; if it does, I will handle it when it happens; if it does not happen, I will not waste my time in anxiety and worry.

Dale Carnegie's classic *How to Stop Worrying and Start Living*[2] makes this point by telling a story: a man giving a commencement address advises students to live their lives in "day-tight compartments." The phrase is derived from U.S. Navy ships under battle conditions operating with watertight compartments. In case of damage, each compartment's hatches were sealed to maintain watertight integrity. Damage and water would be contained within the locked-down (dogged-down) compartment.

The speaker's point: he had learned to live in day-tight compartments, to let each day stand as a separate life. He had learned never to carry over—from one day to the next—worries and fears, and never to project them into the days ahead. "Each day has enough trouble of its own."

As Norman Vincent Peale often said, "I know of no other way to live without worry and fear than to *hold* and *practice* the belief that God will take care of me." This is the secret of the ancients, as well as today's most effective people: view each day as a separate life.

A woman, deeply disturbed by the death of her husband and having no means of support, took a job selling encyclopedias. The job required much lonely driving. She felt great anxiety and uncertainty about the future. One night, she stopped at a small hotel, picked up a magazine in the reading room and saw these words: "Every day is a new life to a wise man." She cut this sentence out and pasted it on the dashboard of her car. Nothing ever helped her as much as these few words. She began to live by them, to consider each day as a new life, a gift from God... a complete unit.[3]

A businessman used a daily ritual to remind himself to take it one day at a time. Leaving the office at 5:00 p.m., he would tear off the day's date from the wall calendar, crumple it up, and pray, *Dear Lord, you have been with me throughout this day. I have done the best I can. You have helped me immensely. Where I have done well, it has been you working through me; where I have failed, I have failed to listen to you. Help me to do better tomorrow; but this day, I leave behind in your hands. Make it what you will. Tonight I'm going to relax and rejoice in the events of this evening, in your name.* Then he would toss the crumpled-up calendar page into the wastebasket, turn off the light, lock the door, and leave the day consciously behind him.

To live in day-tight compartments is to seal each day as if it were a ship's compartment. The secret of life is to think of each day as a separate life. No carryover from yesterday; therefore, no guilt. No projection into the future; therefore, no fear.

¿Para hoy? (For today?)

Yes. I have no life beyond today.

Chapter 15

More Certain Joys

What were the best days of your life?

Maybe you think of the best days as yet to come. But in the past, what stands out? What immediately is formed in the mind are the days when satisfaction was complete—the days of perfection, excitement, exhilaration. The days of sublime emotional highs are instantly recalled.

I remember once looking in the mirror. I was twenty-five years old. I owned a business. I owned a Porsche. I was in the Virgin Islands to lead a five-man scuba dive on the wreck, *The Rhone*, where the movie *The Deep* was filmed. I was tanned, prepared and felt totally competent. I had organized this dive and planned every detail. The expedition into the British Virgin Islands to uninhabited Salt Island, the dive site, was a demonstration of precise research.

Around the turn of the nineteenth century, *The Rhone* had hit a reef in a hurricane, plunging over a hundred souls to a stormy, terrifying death. The hulk lay, like a loaf of French bread broken in half, in fifty feet of transparent, shimmering water. The other half sloped gradually into ninety feet of water. Schools of colorful, exotic fish hid in small compartments of the broken ship, using it as sanctuary from larger predators—their little glimmering selves flaunting a true panorama of marine life.

Because of the dive's depth, planning for a safe return involved lines dropped to the ocean floor, air tanks tied at intervals for decompression stops, back-up air tanks, refueling locations, anticipated possible weather changes and shark strategies. My U.S. Navy training had included the maxim of the sea and the wisdom of the old salts: "An adventure at sea is a penalty for poor planning."

Our group had adventures that day, but not as the result of poor planning. We rescued a diver from another boat panicked by malfunctioning equipment. We had an unbelievable two dives with a great lunch in-between—and possibly saved a life. We had done it all. On the way back, we stopped for refueling at an exclusive British Virgins Yacht Club, had a drink, and told the story of the day's adventures. The experience couldn't have been any better.

Back at the hotel in St. Thomas, all the scuba gear washed, dried, and stowed, I showered and looked at the bronzed image in the mirror. I thought, *I would be content to look this way, feel this way and be this person for the rest of my life. I wouldn't ask anything more.*

But as we know, life doesn't work that way. I went back to my job after the vacation. I changed. The world changed. As the saying goes, you never step into the same river twice. Life changed things around me and within me. Time flows through the corridors of memory and meaning, the scenes change, life settles into a baseline, and *The Rhone* becomes an unforgettable Roman candle display.

Charlie Brown's Lucy expresses it for all of us: "Why does life have to be ups and downs? Why can't it be all *ups*? Why can't we go from an *up* to an *upper up*?"

Good question.

The answer may be in our desire to control the wild cards. *If I could just arrange everything the way it should be, the way I want it to be. If I could write the story, hire the actors and musicians, direct the cast, conduct the orchestra, I could make it perfect; then I could hear the applause, then I could be secure. Then I would be happy.*

You'd think people in positions of absolute power would be able to "get everything right"—arrange people, circumstances, and conditions and produce happiness. Napoleon Bonaparte was in full, uncontested control of his world. Feared, powerful, seemingly unbeatable—he should have been the happiest of men.

"Napoleon had everything men usually crave—glory, power, riches—yet he said, 'I have never known six happy days in my life.'"[1]

A famous ruler, a king with immense wealth and privilege, beauty all around, everything at his command, had the absolute and unchallenged power of life and death residing within him. He once calculated the number of truly happy days in over forty years of rule: the number was thirteen.

This king, with the ability to arrange everything to his complete satisfaction—to orchestrate the days of his life and achieve the ultimate personal fulfillment—could only recall thirteen days of complete happiness. *If that's true, what chance have I got?*

Probably none, especially if we factor in the bad days. There are days of minor discouragement and depression, but there are also days of trauma, days of tragedy, disillusionment and hopelessness. Death, doom, and excessive misery. Only highs and lows: this is our lot. Jerked around between two extremes—ecstasy or excrement. Please, these are the only options in the plan of a loving, caring God?

It's time to consider the "absolute gem of the average day." That phrase has been permanently etched in my mind. I don't remember where I first came across it. It abides with me to this day, mostly because it centered an immense truth in my conscious awareness. The average day, the day that brings no high highs or low lows, is the profoundly satisfying frame. This space has no exhilaration, no exhumation. Nothing to recommend it, except that it is lived, complete with duty, choices, the release of stretched-out futures and anticipated minor joys. It is lived with pleasures near at hand, easily acquired. Joys less demanding; joys unspeakable, joys full of unexpressed glory, taken for granted. Quiet, accepted, and at the same time unexpected. Joys more certain.

More certain joys. This phrase is drawn with great respect from a letter sent to famed essayist E. B. White from his father, Samuel White: "If you feel you are lacking in ambition, be assured that meditation (and contemplation)...is a more certain joy in life...anyone can indulge ambition. Only those who have the spirit can revel in passive enjoyment."[2] What incredible insight, what unusual advice from a father!

This is the missing ingredient, the unvalued element, the unknown potential of modern life: the permission we give ourselves to *be*. Important is the value we place on the time to reflect, to consider, speculate, to indulge in the unhurried consideration of life's meaning and events. The result can be the sense of the eternal and the serenity that surrounds endeavors of this sort. *Oh, the profound peace of great libraries, museums, galleries, churches, and laboratories....*

For most of us, the average day holds only the promise of a portion of these elements but they are there, nevertheless. Time to reflect, to ponder, to consider, to evaluate. These things were part of the average day before all-consuming entertainment and the technology that drives it—and us. The day was usually devoid of high highs and low lows, but it had a natural rhythm: "To everything there is a season, and a time to every purpose under the heaven: A time to be born, and a time to die; a time to plant, and a time to (harvest) that which is planted...a time to weep, and a time to laugh...a time to mourn, and a time to dance...a time to embrace...a time to love...."[3]

A rural setting strongly supports a natural rhythm, but people often don't feel or notice it. Perhaps hard work gets in the way, without the reflection that accompanies the rest, the break, the glass of ice-cold—and I mean *ice-cold* lemonade—and the accompanying gossip. But even in the city, when the kids are picked up from school, ballet, karate, soccer, football, baseball, basketball, band, detention, friend's house...there is happy chatter all around. Nothing spectacular; just average, ordinary, deeply-satisfying moments—if we open ourselves to them.

The average day is more than all aspects being neutral, without anguish, or peace as the absence of conflict; it's the presence of *awareness*. Beyond the important, the cataclysmic, the vital, the urgent, and certainly beyond the superficial, the average day cries out for recognition. Meaning asserts itself lest there be wistful highs or depressing lows we want to forget. And the only other possibility is plain vanilla days stuffed into a cardboard life we can not taste.

Everyday life can be insightful; it can be instructive, it can be sweet, it can be a time to savor. Of course, we would have to learn the art of savoring, to "give ourselves to the enjoyment of."

We would have to give ourselves to the enjoyment of the preparation and taste our food instead of the rapid unconscious consumption that characterizes our mealtimes. Instead of being at the trough, we can be "at table," as the British say. We have missed most of the meals we have eaten because they have been "media meals." We missed them, but we caught the news, or some silly sit-com on television. Family conversation at mealtimes has all but passed away; dining tables are showpieces for visitors; the family eats on TV trays. My mother was right: it's best if there be no electronic devices operating at mealtimes. Our family ate together; we talked, listened, and learned. Mealtimes were an important part of our education. We belonged and we were wanted. We had a place at the table. We had a place, and our peace is always in our place.

Whatever you think of Ralph Nader's consumer advocacy, you have to admire the close ties forged at mealtimes during his childhood when everyone in his family, young and old, was expected to bring to the table something learned that day, and be prepared to discuss it. The family was not only a school, but it was a resource, an intellectual bank.

"The children," Nathra (Ralph's father) says, "were made to understand that the family was a bank. They put in work, duty, trust. Then they could take out what a child must have—education."[4]

You were listened to, your opinions mattered, and even in a large family, you made an important contribution. Family is not just a word, it is an action verb.

"We grew up in a family where 'things' were never important," says Nader's sister, Claire. "No one in the family collected possessions. We were more interested in ideas."[5]

Deliberately adding reading and reflection to our day helps us find more certain joys. Thinking—and its fuel, reading—is fast becoming a lost art; it is not even rewarded in our schools. Scanning condensed information on computer screens is not real reading. But words are the limits of our knowledge and, therefore, our wisdom. Instead of television gossip or entertainment, we can read for knowledge and wisdom. No crisis compels us; no monetary gain motivates us. We read, and our lives begin to subsume and resonate on a deeper level, lives no longer lived ten miles wide and an inch deep.

Even one day can contain more than one day's wisdom, more than one day's memories. Looking back over lives I know anything about, I can see that most of our days are good days. That there are tragic days and euphoric days there can be no doubt; usually these days are few. The vast majority of our days are uneventful, unremarkable; their moments flow seamlessly and quietly, and need only that we notice them, value them, savor them. *"Only those with the spirit can revel in passive enjoyment...."*

We are mostly too busy to notice, or we long for exciting, triumphant experiences. If we are thoughtful people, we can see the perfect gem aspect of the average day. They pass all too quickly; a lifetime goes by as if it were a sequence of flashing images moving across memory—like the pack of cards we used to riffle through, watching the characters move in a jerky, primitive story.

Falling in love with the average day means deliberately living by living more deliberately. The average day is God's gift to a burdened and weary mankind. It can be filled with devotion and holiness, revered for the very presence of its Creator. It is the dear end of the near end of God...his hand and loving care extended...giving us *this day* our daily bread—the sacrament of this average, common, everyday day.

This day may not be an exhilarated high, or a day of great accomplishment, but without a doubt it is a more frequent day, it is a more dependable day; it is a good day...a more certain joy.

Chapter 16

. . . .

A Time for Everything

"There is a time for everything...under heaven..."
—Ecclesiastes 3:1

"Evil cannot permanently organize itself."
—Dr. Martin Luther King, Jr.

In the entire history of the world, the forces of evil have never been able to maintain a forward momentum, even though their activities are ongoing and constant.

This apparent paradox can only be resolved by examining the record of history. In each event, the tyrant or dictator has overplayed his hand, gone too far, lost balance and the ability to reason, and fallen victim to his (or her) overweening success.

The bow—more powerful the further it is drawn back—drawn back too far, shatters without warning and becomes powerless.

Human affairs reflect this: to push and push, to want something too much, to go too far, to press too hard, to overemphasize, place too great a value on one thing as opposed to another—ultimately to find that the thing greatly desired is lost. This is a common experience.

The God of the universe is a God of order, and a big part of order is *balance*. All things in their season, and there is a season for all things.

Anything that is out of balance is out of order, and that includes too much of anything. The ancients extolled the virtues of what was called the *golden mean*, a reference to the beauty of the middle ground. Not the worship or ultimate glorification of mediocrity, but the importance of not overemphasizing any one good thing to the detriment of others, which would invariably lead to the penalties of excess. Choice morsels of good food are very desirable, but too much ends in gluttony and obesity. Too little—an extreme in the opposite direction—leads to malnutrition, anemia, susceptibility to disease, and premature death. "Wine…gladdens the heart of man…"[1] but drunkenness dissolves the true personality—along with character, reputation, and eventually, health.

While these are physical examples of small import, the issue goes deeper. As Mahatma Gandhi was quoted as saying, "When I despair, I remember that all through history the way of truth and love has always won. There have been tyrants and murderers and for a time they seemed invincible but in the end, they always fall—think of it…*always*." Those who perpetuate evil have, for a time, appeared to succeed, but then become infatuated with success. They become top-heavy; they fall over and disintegrate. A now-famous photograph symbolizes this truth: broken and disfigured, a statue of Stalin in a Moscow park has fallen on its side. The statue's finger, once pointing sternly to the sky, now points ludicrously off to one side. The overall effect is a caricature of fierce, prideful malevolence now rendered humorously harmless. Stupid, even.

> I met a traveler from an antique land
> Who said:—Two vast and trunkless legs of stone
> Stand in the desert. Near them on the sand,
> Half sunk, a shatter'd visage lies, whose frown
> And wrinkled lip and sneer of cold command
> Tell that its sculptor well those passions read

Which yet survive, stamp'd on these lifeless things,
The hand that mock'd them and the heart that fed.
And on the pedestal these words appear:
"My name is Ozymandias, king of kings:
Look on my works, ye mighty, and despair!"
Nothing beside remains: round the decay
Of that colossal wreck, boundless and bare,
The lone and level sands stretch far away.
                                   —Percy Bysshe Shelley[2]

Evil has been unmasked through all these dissolving moments. More than just what is known as morally wrong, evil is revealed as a possible good taken to an impossible extreme, pushed out of shape, falling over because it can no longer keep its balance.

Too much work, too much play, too much entertainment, too much of too much, and the universal reversal effect moves in.

Think of the consummate balance in nature, the seasons, the rhythm of the day. A time for work, a time for play, a time for rest, a time for planting, a time for harvesting, a time for *everything*, with nothing to the exclusion of all else. An exquisite balance is maintained, each phase leading into the next with smooth, unstudied perfection.

We do not often think of things out of balance as evil. But when we think of evil and see that it essentially is *good* stretched beyond its rightful place, our perception becomes different. This is also Satan's dilemma: all that involves reason, understanding, order, and the 'good' belong to God. Only the opposites belong to Satan: unreason, misunderstanding, disorder, and the 'bad.' The problem of rebellion is that the rebel is left with only that which is unwanted and unclaimed. Evil can make a fearsome start, threaten, appear invincible and awesome, but cannot maintain these conditions. Inevitably, because it is left with only the opposite of the good (that is, the permanent), it begins to unravel and disintegrate because rebellion is *impermanent*.

In a universe founded on justice, truth, and good, there is only that which is reality, i.e., *real*; the opposite would have to be what is *unreal*, illusory, transitory, impermanent.

Along with beauty, along with truth, along with order, let us cultivate *balance*. If we lose our balance, we fall. This is what sin really is: we lose our balance, and we fall. God restores us to equilibrium—and with it, peace. We regain our balance, and are calmed...serene; order is restored.

All that is evil, all that is rebellion, all that is anti-God, is destined for the lake of fire.

That is its destination; it is out of order.

Chapter 17

In This World

"I have told you these things, so that in me you may have peace. In this world you will have trouble. But take heart! I have overcome the world."

—John 16:33

When difficulties or tragedy become part of our lives, it is only natural to question God's care of us. It is only natural to question his *ability* to care for us. What could possibly be his motive in allowing something to happen that we did not want to happen? Doesn't God love us? Does he want us to suffer?

In the film *Shadowlands*, British writer and Christian theologian C.S. Lewis is quoted as saying, "What if the answer to that question is 'yes?' I'm not sure that God particularly wants us to be happy. He wants us to love and be loved. He wants us to grow up. I suggest to you that it is because God loves us that he makes us the gift of suffering. Pain is God's megaphone to rouse a deaf world." [1]

What if God doesn't want us to be happy? What a shocker! What if the American ideal—the pursuit of happiness—is not God's plan? He doesn't want us to be happy? Is that possible?

The problem is with the word *happiness*.

No matter how many people we asked, no two would describe happiness in the same way. They might even be polar opposites in their conceptions. For one, happiness might be peace and quiet; for another, happiness might be activity, accomplishment, thrills.

For many, though, happiness might be something like security, not lacking anything, everything in life at a hundred percent and staying that way forever. But that's a definition of heaven, not this world. No financial insecurity, for example: "But I thought if I did the right things, I would lose my financial insecurity," a young man told his mentor. "I said you would lose your *fear* of financial insecurity," the older man said. "You're going to be financially insecure all of your life, son; everybody is. Just don't be afraid of it."

Wise man. If you put your trust in God to take care of you, you may be financially insecure, but you won't be afraid. If you try to remove the financial insecurity once and for all, no matter how much money you have, you will try to keep from losing it; the attempt alone will create fear. Then add attempts to make your kids perfect, your health perfect, your relationships…fear will rule your life. No happiness there.

> "I think I already understand about life: pretty good, some problems."[2]
>
> —Sam Lamott, age 7

It's not going to be perfect in this world. There is plenty here to encourage us, lots of fun if we know how to find it, love if we know how to give it, beauty if we can absorb it—and some trouble. It just reminds us that this world is not our home, and our only real, lasting treasure is Christ. *"I have told you these things, so that in me you may have peace."*

Chapter 18

Notes from Home

"Gather up the fragments... that nothing be lost."
—John 6:12, KJV

These 'reminders from heavenly places' are encapsulated versions of some of my teaching themes throughout the years:

The purposes of your life are worked out through reaching out, not arriving at some destination.

To be conformed to the pattern of this world is to be conformed to an illusion. You will never know who or what you are.

God's will is not like a slot-car track—rigid, unyielding determination to perform. God's will is more like a big playground, with creative combinations everywhere, kids to have fun with—and protective barriers at the edges to keep you from going over the cliff.

God does not reveal his plans, but tells us how to live so that his plans can be accomplished in us. He positions us for fulfillment.

In the spiritual life, you "tear off your own strip." *You* decide how much of the kingdom of God you will inherit, how much will function in and through you. "The kingdom of heaven has endured violent assault, and violent men seize it by force [as a precious prize…]"[1]

God does not have favorites, but he does have intimates.

Satan is a great impulse activator; urging us to act without praying, decide without examining, move without seeking God. If we are being pressed to pursue solutions without pursuit of God, it is always the enemy.

Humility is really *teachability*: the willingness to learn from God, to depend on him. The opposite of humility is not so much pride, as pride's result: self-sufficiency.

If you separate *religion* from *life*, you become two-faced, hypocritical—because you must then use two different value systems.

The Bible tells you that God loves you; everybody knows that—
or should. But do you think that God *likes* you? Love can be a
generic term, vague and nonspecific. God knows everything I've
done and thought, so how could he possibly like me? But you
can't *love* someone and not *like* them. God likes you, and the
implications of that are enormous.

When in doubt, do the loving thing. You will always be right in
God's eyes, even if others misunderstand. Love is the sum of all
the law and the prophets. "Love does no wrong to anyone. That's
why it fully satisfies all of God's requirements. It is the only law
you need."[2]

We're just people. No matter how hard we try, we never rise
above basic human being. It's good to progress, but failing to
remember the context can make us despairing.

Radical Thought No. 1:

To make God happy, we need to learn to receive. There is more
teaching in the Bible—and more examples—of receiving than of
giving. Both are important. We can give, and in so doing, give
ourselves pleasure; but if we cannot receive, we cannot give God
pleasure. "Fear not, little flock; for it is your Father's good
pleasure to give you the kingdom."[3]

To "go with the flow" is a popular saying; it implies ease, un-
concern about strife, things will just happen by themselves—no
worries, mate. But the phrase contains a poison pill, an intrinsic
fallacy that can be extremely misleading and harmful. First ask,
"Where is the flow going?" Is its destination Christ-approved?

We can go along with events and the opinions of others, the actions of our peer group, those whose opinion we respect, and the general expectations of everyone. God calls us, at times, to go against the flow of this world—the "normal" Christian life, the opinions of others, and the general expectations of aggressive people. Forget about the flow; go with God. Only dead fish go with the flow.

Radical Thought No. 2:

Should a Christian be deceptive, aggressive, hostile and misrepresent the truth? If you said "no," you would be within the majority opinion. But pastors and counselors get questions like this: "In my job as a police officer, I am sometimes required to do all these things, and as an undercover officer, I know I must ultimately betray people who have trusted me. Should I quit my job and work in a Christian environment?" My answer: "The struggle you have is the very thing that honors God; otherwise, many people in law enforcement are likely to be non-caring people who enjoy inflicting pain, people who are not bothered by or wrestle with the conditions you describe. Stay in your job. God will tell you if and when it's time to move on."

Peace is not the highest or deciding value, but we often think it is: "I have a peace about it." But peace can come as a result of the *end of conflict*—good giving in to evil, forsaking God's principles and surrendering to Satan's schemes. Conflict ends; now we have "peace." This is a false peace. Following God's way sometimes means unrest, sacrifice, unsettledness. God's will is not always immediately pleasurable; God's will is always ultimately pleasurable.

"The desires of your heart"[4] are the key to your future because God put them there. He did so because he intends to fulfill them.

The power of interpretation is part of the art of life. Events do not have an intrinsic or irrevocable meaning. *I* decide the meaning of events in my life. God's view of me is more important than conventional wisdom, my guilt or fears, the perception of others, or the non-interpretation of the passive view. I learn to "reframe" events to fit the perspective God provides.

Chapter 19

Stop Loss Orders

I can't win for losing."

Most of us have heard or spoken this phrase at one time or another and it contains a certain truth: often the fastest way to turn a bad situation around is to *first* stop losing. This truth is reflected in the well-known Twelve-Step program slogan, "If you're in a hole, stop digging." A valuable tool in the world of stock investments is known as a stop loss order. This simple device triggers the sale of the stock if its value declines to a predetermined point. The stock is automatically sold at that price, limiting the loss. "It's possible to be wrong over half the time and still make money, when you utilize the stop-loss order," said a leading investor. This can be a valuable life principle as well.

The Bible mandates a limit to certain relationships. "Blessed is the man who does not walk in the counsel of the wicked or stand in the way of sinners or sit in the seat of mockers,"[1] the psalmist observes. The Old Testament book of Proverbs and the New Testament both warn us against exposing ourselves to evil and corrupting influences; clearly we should limit or sever relationships with abrasive, aggressive, "toxic" personalities.

This is especially true if we are in the position of protection where women or children are concerned; tender spirits are easily wounded. The offender is sometimes a critical relative, someone who likes to belittle and dominate through intimidation. A husband may have to step in to protect his wife from harsh, demeaning treatment by a service or repairperson.

We must teach our dating teenagers that what people *do* is what is really meant, not necessarily what is *said*. Someone who tells you that they care for you, but verbally or physically abuses you is demonstrating the real nature of their feeling. "I believed him when he said he loved me," one woman wrote about her husband, "even though he beat me and sexually abused me. He said it was *my* fault, that I made him crazy, that he was insanely jealous, that it was because he loved me so much. I thought if I tried harder, things would get better. It was a long time before I realized the truth."

While this is an extreme case, it demonstrates how hard it can be to draw a line, to stop the loss. Admitting mistakes is hard; we have invested much time and effort in this relationship. In the world of the stock market, this is called the Previous Investment Trap ("I've had this stock for a long time, and I'm emotionally attached to the company; it's bound to increase in value. The stock has always gone up before...").

We're not concerned with stocks and bonds here, but simply applying the principle of stopping the loss, or setting limits to negative situations. We can do this in other areas of life, not just investments and relationships. A friend of mine puts a stop loss order on waiting for people who are late. I discovered this the hard way when I was late for a lunch meeting, and ran into him in the parking lot as he was leaving. He explained, politely, that I had passed his fifteen-minute limit, wasting his time and mine. We did have lunch that day, but I was never late in meeting him again. A recent *Dilbert* cartoon advises us to "Always postpone meetings with time-wasting morons." When one of the cartoon characters asks, "How do I do that?" The answer was, "Let me get back to you on that." [2]

One of the most valuable applications of this principle is placing a stop-loss order on minor hassles, especially over money. The author of an article written years ago related his decision to stop fretting over any amount of twenty dollars or less—to just let it go, whether it was incorrect change, money left over from a purchase, or money lost in a variety of ways. "I found that it eliminated dozens of small irritations. When my fortunes increased, I raised the amount and removed more unhappiness. Then I began to apply it to things other than money; if it was small and inconsequential, I just let it go.

"Slights, chance remarks, inconsiderate actions, unmet expectations—you can't believe how this principle improved the quality of my life. I became a cheerful, easy-going, forgiving person; someone others liked to have around. I was not only happier, but as you can imagine, it was great for business."

Putting a stop-loss order on worries is a good idea, too. *I will concern myself with these problems, and no more. I will clearly define the problem, write down possible solutions, pray about it, and turn it over to my loving heavenly Father.* Philippians 4:6-7 reflects this tender assurance from the Lord: "Do not be anxious about anything, but in everything, by prayer and petition, with thanksgiving, present your requests to God. And the peace of God, which transcends all understanding, will guard your hearts and your minds in Christ Jesus."

A Christian may sometimes be called to a situation in which fearful people are lashing out, or destructive impulses are acted upon. Should we walk away from hurting people if they are abusive? Of course not; but it is vital to be in a ministry stance. Approach them prayerfully, try to help if possible, never sink to their level, and never take personally what they say or do.

A stop-loss order is a way of setting limits. A successful life is always lived within the boundaries of God's Word; his message is to keep us from all harm.

Chapter 20

Not a Bribe— a Belonging

We come to God to get *his* way, not our way.

This statement underlies Christian commitment. We have tried *our* way; it has left us with the taste of ashes and the emptiness of loss. This is especially true where giving is concerned.

It's not a question of how we are used to giving. It is not how others give, or what we may have been taught about giving. The question is—what does God want? The answer may be surprising.

There is a sequence of giving. First, we give to God. Not just money, but ourselves. Mark 12:30 makes clear the priority: to love the Lord your God with *all*...heart, soul, mind, and strength. This is the first commandment.

Second—and this is the shocker: we give to ourselves. We love others *as we do ourselves.* We make an investment in our lives through Bible study, worship, education, growth, time to think and reason, and accomplishment that leads to advancement. The person who has little or nothing has little or nothing to give.

Third, we give to others as we ourselves have received. As we expand through the investment in our own lives, we include others in the circle of receiving. Many things are promised; many things are accomplished by living within this sequence.

One of the most important accomplishments comes as we teach ourselves, at the most basic level, there is nothing to fear. Giving is one of the ultimate acts of release from future anxiety. *There is plenty; I do not need to hoard, to store up in barns, to worry about tomorrow or the day after.* This is a message we send to ourselves; we receive it in the deepest part of our being.

God's Word stipulates that we are to give freely, without restraint. This is rarely understood because we often feel compelled to give. The compulsion takes place in the form of emotional appeals for money; barters, threats, and heart-rending stories of massive need are part of the pressure used. But if you are forced to give, you can't give. Giving is a gift; it's voluntary, planned, and done with joy. The heavy atmosphere of emotional blackmail in many church services or charitable appeals negates the whole idea of a gift, and carries the overtones of guilt, or a purchase of God's favor.

The Bible's directive is that giving should be a cheerful, voluntary act. Each person, on a planned and regular basis, should decide what gifts to give and then act accordingly. Given the leveraged appeals of some televangelists, churches, and mass mailings from fund-raisers, what has been presented as giving is actually extortion; in some cases, it becomes payment for healing, God's favor, the release of guilt, or goods and services.

This extortion category also applies to "gifts" given with strings attached. An acquaintance of mine had an extremely wealthy father, founder of a nation-wide chain of retail stores—a tycoon in every sense. He informed his son that he had just written a check for one million dollars to his church. Medium-sized and denominational, the church had never received an amount of this magnitude. The father told his son of the requirements, the stipulations he had made, and what he wanted the church to do with the money; in effect, he wanted to buy control of the enterprise, just as he was used to doing in business. His son, a strong and committed Christian, replied, "Dad, did you ever just *give* anything?"

The tithe should be given to God by giving to his work. This ten percent of income is part of God's plan, and there are great rewards promised to those who are a part of it. Great rewards, "pressed down, shaken together, and running over"[2] will be given. Giving is not limited to money alone; time, energy, talent, and creativity are included in the directive, "Give, and it will be given to you, for with the measure you use, it will be measured to you..."[3] A *measure* was the unit of measurement, or "scoop" used in biblical times to measure grain. In terms of what comes back to me—in all ways—I get to choose the scoop by the one I choose in giving. But it's not a bribe; it's a belonging.

That's worth repeating. *It's not a bribe; it's a belonging.* Only the hired hands are paid every week. Sons and daughters belong to the family; the family enterprise belongs to them. They are the owners; the children are the inheritors. In the meantime, they receive what they need. They belong to the enterprise; the enterprise belongs to them.

All Scripture taken together expresses the very nature of giving; it cannot be forced, manipulated, stipulated with strings attached; it cannot be a barter arrangement, a bribe, or a payment, or it's not giving. If you *have to* give, then you can't give, any more than you can be forced to love. If you are forced in any way to give, it can't be a gift.

I can count on God's love being free and unrestrained, not earned or forced out of him. If I am part of his plan, the benefits will be returned to me—and multiplied—over that vast scale of human and divine enterprise called life.

Chapter 21

The Royal Law...Love Myself?

"If you really keep the royal law found in Scripture, 'Love your neighbor as yourself,' you are doing right."

—James 2:8

What the apostle James calls "The Royal Law" certainly requires loving others, but uses a standard most of us have never been comfortable with: loving our *self*. The Bible makes an assumption that we have a basic approval and affirmation of ourselves, and directs us to *use* it to approve and affirm others we come into contact with.

Dr. Smiley Blanton, a Christian psychiatrist noted for his down-home, earthy good sense, once said, "It's as plain as the nose on your face. The solution to life is love. The ability to love comes from loving ourselves, and extends outwardly to enclose others." He knew what he was talking about. This principle is stated at least ten times in Scripture—starting in Leviticus and endorsed by Jesus himself, the apostle Paul, and continuing through the book of James.

The point made by Dr. Blanton—questions of self-doubt and sometimes profound self-dislike—forms the basis of many of our difficulties and physical ailments. It is also at the root of why we find it difficult to love other people.

This will help: you know that God *loves* you, but do you think God *likes* you?

Most people believe that God loves them. The Bible tells them so. But they have a hard time believing that God *likes* them, because they know their areas of defeat and failure. *How could God, who is perfect and pure, like someone who thinks some of the things I think, let alone the things I have done? How could a holy God approve of me, affirm me, like me enough to want to hang out with me?*

Here's the answer: you can't love someone—following the biblical definition of love found in the thirteenth chapter of Corinthians—and not like them.

> "Love is very patient and kind, never jealous or envious, never boastful or proud, never haughty or selfish or rude. Love does not demand its own way. It is not irritable or touchy. It does not hold grudges and will hardly even notice when others do it wrong. It is never glad about injustice, but rejoices whenever truth wins out. If you love someone you will be loyal to him no matter what the cost. You will always believe in him, always expect the best of him, and always stand your ground in defending him."[1]

In the whole idea of love is the idea of approval, the sense of affirming and caring, the desire to be with them. *If God doesn't like us, he doesn't love us.* If God rejects us, we reject all others and ourselves; we take it out on them. We have to. If we are the standard, the baseline, there is no other choice. But God doesn't reject us. Far from it. "For God so loved the world (us), that he gave his one and only Son...." The familiar words from John 3:16 enclose us.

Inside of each of us, God has placed a sense of sacredness. We are prone to reject that sacredness—disregard it, cover it up with sins, failures and disappointments. We then pronounce ourselves worthless and impossible to redeem. The part of us that makes connection with God is rejected as well.

People make mistakes, commit sins. As Christians, these mistakes and sins may not be as serious as we think. They are of importance, they grieve God; but they are of a different nature than the same offenses committed by those who hate God. The angry mob *outside* the house may throw a rock and break a window; the kids who live *inside* the house may throw a football and break a window. In both cases there is a broken window. But the *nature* of the break is vastly different; the owner of the house cannot view these two events as the same. The angry mob outside the house must first end rebellion and enmity. The broken window is a violent expression of that hatred and opposition towards the owner of the house.

The "owner of the house" is, of course, God. The child who breaks the window is his own flesh and blood. If the child has broken a rule, or law, there is a remedy for that: confession and receiving his Father's forgiveness. We must believe in and accept God's forgiveness for the broken window—or law; otherwise, we set ourselves up as a higher court than God himself. "What God has cleansed, call that not unclean."[2]

When we feel clean, valuable, and empowered, we naturally extend those qualities into the day's activities and the people we meet. We treat others as we have already treated ourselves.

If we separate from the sense of sacredness inside, we separate from our help. If we have rejected God's opinion of us, we have rejected his perception of us in Christ. When we end this separation, we rise to a higher plane, with a much greater degree of success. There will be growth, the end of failure in any permanent sense, and deep empathy for others.

It begins with a profound confidence of our own worth in God's eyes, and that worth means *I approve of what God approves of…me.*

Chapter 22

Safe Within the Circle

…Glowing eyes in the dark; the predators prowl, watching for an opportunity to attack…the protective circle of the glowing campfire; safe within, a festive- meal is prepared and enjoyed…*in the presence of my enemies…*

Because the Lord is my Shepherd,
    I have everything I need!
He lets me rest in the meadow grass
    and leads me beside the quiet streams.
He gives me new strength.
He helps me to do what honors him the most.
Even when walking through the dark valley of death
    I will not be afraid,
    for you are close beside me,
    guarding, guiding all the way.
You provide delicious food for me
    in the presence of my enemies.
You have welcomed me as your guest;
    blessings overflow!

Your goodness and unfailing kindness
shall be with me all of my life,
and afterwards I will live with you forever in your home.[1]

The powerful imagery of king David's poem of praise—what we know as the Twenty-third Psalm—brings the most loved psalm to vivid life. David's enemies were prowling around, seeking opportunity to pounce and devour, but David was safe within the circle of God's protection and care. More than safe, a feast was provided—even in the presence of his enemies. The picture emerges as one of almost quiet taunting. The predators, helpless to attack, are watched contemplatively; the feast is greatly enjoyed.

Circle of power; circle of dependence on his Father; circle of love.

David, the consummate poet-warrior, was certainly loved by the Father and described as a man after God's own heart.[2] In every circumstance—especially when David had sinned or failed—he turned to God for help, forgiveness, cleansing, and protection. He sought perfection in God, not in himself. He was also a man of prayer; this is evident from the number of David's prayers that were written down and preserved for us. David's prayers are powerful because no matter how badly he had failed, he never assumed he was permanently separated from God.

David understood that prayer is first of all relationship. Before prayer becomes words, or ritual, or forms, or classic phrases, it is assumed intimacy—intimacy that is initiated by God and accepted by man. Your father is always your father; you are always his son or daughter, no matter what you do or don't do. Nothing can change that.

Satan vividly demonstrated the issue of relationship and intimacy with the Father in the account of Jesus' temptation in the wilderness. The underlying premise of Satan's attack is the attempt to create doubt concerning Jesus' relationship to the Father; to question the bloodline, to deny the family tie: "If you are the Son of God…" and then follows the specific temptation: turn stones into bread, throw yourself down from the temple—to use material

110

things for personal, selfish benefit; to achieve quick results through sensational means.[3] Satan's attempt at placing doubt was useless; Jesus knew who he was.

Your own identity as a beloved child of God is always the question, always the challenge, always the basis for the tempter's snare: "*If* you are the son / daughter of God...." There will be times when you must know who you are—not your name, your Social Security number, or what you do for a living; times when we see the glowing eyes of circling evil, the purveyors of hopeless news—in the dark hospital corridor, in the banker's office; the presentation of hopelessness and despair—in the implosion of a relationship, in the test results, uniformed persons knocking on your front door; in the personal failures—the slaughter of hopes and dreams...everything that makes sense or ever could make sense has flown away on the wings of a dragon—not on the wings of a snow white dove.

We need our Father. We need to pray.

Prayer is involvement with the supernatural; it elects to interfere. Prayer is based on the assumption that something needs to be changed, and that something is beyond the will or the ability of human beings. Prayer is interfering; it is re-arranging; it is re-directing, it is re-sequencing events. *Things are going in the wrong direction, and I'm going to change that direction.*

Through involvement with the supernatural power of God in prayer, we gradually become more familiar with and trusting in that which defies logic. We begin to have faith in what defies the rational. This is vital. Things that can be changed by man—through man's natural means—do not need God's intervention. If we can blast a hole through the mountain with dynamite and build a railroad, we don't need to ask God to do it supernaturally. But if it is impossible with man, it is still possible with God.[4]

Through prayer, we can go beyond the logical, the rational, the material, the possible. But on what basis? Magic? Formulas and incantations? Certainly not. We can invade the supernatural only on the basis that Jesus performed his miracles: "I do only what I see my Father doing."[5] If we can be shaken from our position as children of God, we can do nothing. What builds our confidence in the Father-child bond? Consistent prayer. Prayer builds our faith, our confidence, our reliance on the supernatural.

Prayer builds our confidence in the supernatural. The supernatural is the power of God. Our use of this power is based on our relationship as "king's kids." The more we pray, the more the Holy Spirit bears witness to our relationship with the Father. The more certain we are of our life as his children, the more God's reality and his answers to prayer overcome our logic in times of need. In turn, our knowledge of who we are in Christ intensifies.

God is most glorified when we trust completely in him; we trust in him when we depend on Him to transcend the logical and transform our need into what makes loving completion. *"Thou preparest a table before me in the presence of mine enemies...."*[6]

Chapter 23

Highest Honor

A muscular arm holding the deadly double-edged sword of the Roman legionnaire slashed down to the neck of the helpless enemy. Certain, bloody death was a split-second away....

Months later, an awards ceremony was held honoring the best, most courageous soldiers of the conquering Roman army. The troops were assembled; following the awards for service, valor, and courage in battle, one final award remained. Who would it be? Who would be the recipient of the highest honor Rome could bestow?

The announcement was a shock. The award went to an ordinary, regular Roman legionnaire for this one simple reason: in the act, in the very split-second of the act of killing an enemy, he heard the trumpet sound withdrawal, and he stopped his sword in mid-air—in mid-stroke—and withdrew.

The highest honor went not to bravery, but to obedience.

By contrast, Abraham Lincoln gave direct orders to General Meade following the Battle of Gettysburg. The orders were simple and explicit: attack General Lee while his Confederate army was pinned between the advancing victorious Union army and the rain-swollen Potomac River. Meade procrastinated, rationalized, and finally flatly disobeyed Lincoln's repeated order. The river subsided and Lee escaped, prolonging the war an agonizing two more years.

In conversation with a member of his cabinet, Lincoln later exclaimed, "Great God! What does this mean? We had them within our grasp. We had only to stretch forth our hands and they were ours. And nothing I could say or do could make the army move."[1]

Victory was lost because of disobedience.

Today's Christianity places a great deal of value on victory, success, winning, and being Number One. Many ads for churches, seminars, tape series, teachings and books stress the idea that being a Christian means winning or succeeding. No one could argue with this concept if success or winning took the long view and was tied to God's will; existing as an isolated concept, it is founded in an appeal to the self-centered desire to control God and events. Success or victory becomes the standard of evaluation, the decision factor, and the sign of God's presence and approval. This is faulty theology and shallow Christianity.

Spiritual writers of times past equated the deepest aspects of Christian life with a word that we are not so familiar with today: *detachment*.

The word refers to a state of mind, of heart, of position, of being—most importantly, of determination. This determination consists of a non-ownership of the end result. The individual is determined to link and relate to Christ as a Person, not as a cause. Obedience is the key; the end result is up to Jesus, the commander of the Lord's army. This is a vital and indispensable difference, and failure to realize and separate these two positions has led to disastrous consequences for people, nations, and Christianity. And it is often done with the best of intentions—for the cause of Christianity.

Once we lose sight of a personal relationship with Christ, it is easy to set up organizations, make plans, formulate procedures and progressive steps to accomplish our goals, organize resources, raise funds—and be completely impervious to the fact that the Holy Spirit turned left five miles back.

We may begin with genuine revelation born of a deep desire to do something great for God. It is also possible to become totally unresponsive to God's fine-tuning, changes, or in some cases, to misinterpret the original revelation and become invulnerable to God's protests and corrections. We can even become the enemies of God.

Consider the following historical examples: both the Inquisition and the Crusades were based originally on the desire to preserve, protect and further the kingdom of God. In the beginning, these were the goals of the Cause of Christ. If anyone with a sincere desire to hear what Christ was saying *personally* had been in a position of leadership, the torture and slaughter of thousands of people would have been avoided.

The point is…Christ is not a cause.

"Christianity," which should only define the ones who follow Christ, can come to mean the "Cause of Christ"—a completely different thing, with the attendant perversions possible.

Devotion to a cause is not the same thing as devotion to Christ. The cause becomes an organization, and organizations have no soul. The shocking truth is that even Christian organizations have no soul; only people have souls. Once an organization is formed, it has stated purposes, objectives, and methodology for attaining these goals. In corporate America, this is the way to run a business. If the organization is led by committed Christians, so much the better. But if we confuse the organization with the person of Christ, we can easily be convinced that Christ is a member of our team, denomination, political party, group, and organization. It is then a short hop to the conviction that he would drive a BMW, wear a Rolex, and endorse the latest Christian celebrity we prefer at the moment, simply because *we* do.

Only the truly detached soul can clearly hear the voice of God. As long as personal motives remain—even the best of personal motives—the self and its coloring ambitions crawl into the framework of perceptions, add holy rationalizations, and denigrate all opposition. *After all, "self" explains, look at the reason I'm doing it; I'm doing it for the cause of Christ. I'm furthering the aims of Christianity. How could that be wrong?*

The Gospel according to Me.

God will surely bless it, and Me, and the sign shall be the number of people I can recruit to my gospel. Success and victory shall be the proof of God's approval, and massive amounts of resources, money, and affirmation from the Christian community shall be my validation. My anointing is certain, my superiority is proven, and I shall not be opposed. God is with me. Who would doubt it in today's world?

Who shall be accorded heaven's highest honor? The person who takes the position that it is the same to sweep floors and have no visible sign of success, as it is to preach to hundreds of thousands. This person is ready to go where Jesus sends them; they are also equally ready *not* to go if it is the Master's will. The things of this world are counted as junk; a different standard applies: "Follow thou me."

Not the song, but the Singer.

Obedience—not victory, success, or the will of the majority—is the hallmark of one who follows Christ. *The sword stops in mid-stroke if the trumpet sounds....*

Highest honor.

Chapter 24

Open on the God-Ward Side

The church today holds tragically-divided, widely-divergent positions on the question of spiritual guidance. One position holds that God still speaks today; the inner voice of the Holy Spirit is the primary source of guidance. The opposing viewpoint sees the excesses and obvious misuse of this so-called guidance and labels it as untrustworthy.

The chasm is enormous. On the one hand, we have the super-radical, mass-researched, market-driven media church festooned with triumphalism. These churches are ornate with show business personalities shown through a television camera's "star lens" to enhance production values. You will hear an excited, "In the name of Jesuuusssss!!!" thrown in periodically for maximum authenticity. Then there is the other extreme: moss-backed, tradition-strangled, tottering, formal, ritualistic institutions dedicated to "Our Lady of Perpetual Repetition." Schedules are big here. The main thing you can count on—in your time of need—is getting out of the service on time. You probably have only heard echoes of God's love from the past; you probably are none the better.

Groups and denominations may hold positions and defend doctrines, but for the individual—when all else fails—there is direct access to God's heart through *discernment*.

There was one unmistakable, very basic condition of the early church: they prayed as if they *knew* God's will. They had no cumbersome infrastructure, no complex hierarchy. As Kierkegaard specified, "Purity of heart is to will one thing,"[1] the church of those early days—without money, status, prestige, or worldly influence—was pure and simple. Armed with discernment, they prayed boldly, not hesitantly or speculatively; not foolishly or flamboyantly; there was none of the prancing "show business" prayers of today's television personalities. The church of the first century prayed with humility, and yet with authority; they drew down the power of God.

God's answer was not always "yes," but it usually was. His "no" was never a refusal. Sometimes it was a redirection. Always God's answer was sought and followed to the best of their ability. Most impressively, the opinions of man were entirely disregarded. Personal safety, monetary stability, relationships, perceptions of others, loss of anything and everything—these were secondary. So secondary it mattered little. What was important was to direct God's power to the needs of others. The men and women of the first century church were unrelentingly "open on the God-ward side."[2] God was what mattered. For the first time in history, the least of men, the least of women—with no official stature—could talk with God directly and know his thoughts. The temple veil separating man from God's presence was torn from top to bottom at the time of the crucifixion. Historians have estimated this veil was thirty feet wide by sixty feet tall, between four to six inches thick. It was so thick and heavy it took four teams of oxen to hang it. The tearing of such a veil could not possibly be the act of a person.

This was intended to be seen as God acting to end the separation between himself and man. Any person in Christ can now approach God directly—without priest, without qualifying, without intermediary, walking confidently into the Holy of Holies to hear from God.

I learned to be "open on the God-ward side" from a man who was a living example of this position. Here's my story:

I have been a pastor, teacher, counselor, writer, and radio broadcaster for over twenty-five years; I have founded two churches and several non-profit ministries. Before this time, I was a businessman, having formed a marketing company serving clients in the Midwest.

Christ came into my life supernaturally in the fall of 1975, through an overpowering urge to leave my office and buy a Bible. While all conversions are supernatural, mine was outside the norm in many ways. I was not attending church, undergoing a particularly difficult time resulting in a "foxhole conversion," or being actively witnessed to by other Christians, although I did have a number of Christian organizations as clients.

That day, I cancelled appointments and went to a nearby bookstore. Wondering at this strange impulse, I bought a Bible and began reading. I found myself saying "yes" to what I was reading. I do not know the day and the hour of my surrender to Christ; I just said, "yes" in some final way, somewhere along the way. Then I knew God wanted me to be a part of a local fellowship of believers, but I didn't have the faintest idea where. Since I was brought up in a mainstream denomination, naturally I rejected it—and God along with it—when I became an all-wise, all-knowing teenager. As a U.S. serviceman, I toured the great cathedrals of Europe. I remember thinking that maybe God was where it was dark and there were a lot of candles.

But that didn't seem to be it. God's sense of rightness eventually led me to a small church and a country pastor whose main activity and ability seemed to be listening to the Holy Spirit. I can't remember any sermon he ever preached, and he was my exact opposite in most social aspects. He was not a literate, educated man; he didn't always "talk real good English," and wore clothes that were out of style and out of shape. But he had this one impressive attribute—to paraphrase Gert Behanna, he was "shiny with the Holy Spirit." He knew how to hear God. He knew a great deal more than that, but that one thing—listening to God—taught him everything else. Those in his church learned to listen to God, but more by example than through sermons. Listening was both a quality he exuded and an ability that he demonstrated. Because of this man's example—from this small church of less than one hundred—more than five churches were planted led by people whose main qualification was listening. He would say things like, "Don't ever become a 'professional,'" meaning if God leads you into ministry, don't rely on systems, structures, and procedures.

Vivid in my memory is the day he came into the church during a weekday (we all had keys to the church!), saw me alone studying the Bible with books spread all around, and said matter-of-factly, "If you keep this up, God will call you." It turns out he was also a prophet—at least concerning me. I had no thoughts of the ministry. I planned to serve Christ as a businessman; ministry was for trained professionals.

I was a draftee, not a volunteer. Being chosen means God supplies certain specific things: guidance, support, and protection for the mission. But I was running a business, not a church. Yet in time, all things necessary came to pass: a Bible study I was "helping out in" became a church, seeking larger and larger quarters, and God did indeed call me, guide me, and protect me as I tried to hear what he was saying. Eventually a church was formed, and I left the business world. My qualifications were simple: the sense of the call itself and its implications, a hunger for God's Word, and the ability—belief—to listen.

I am not Charismatic; neither am I mainstream. At times I feel like an exile from a country whose embassy has been closed for some time. The kingdom of God is a *supernatural* kingdom. Christ's representatives should have access to and rely on the supernatural; ministry should be based on the supernatural. But the special abilities God gives every believer have been relegated to the lunatic fringe or the deadness of the "First Church of the Frigidaire." The gifts are the *gifts of the Holy Spirit*, not the result of study or learned proficiency.

Think of God's spiritual gifts as a car. The Charismatics get in, honk the horn, play with the power windows and stereo, and drive around for fun. They may not use the car for the purpose it was given: to help God's people be, in Keith Miller's phrase, "carriers of the Spirit;" to demonstrate God's willingness to intervene in human need, and thereby help people find him. "You are to be given *power* when the Holy Spirit has come to you. You will be *witnesses* to me, not only in Jerusalem...but to the very ends of the earth."[3] The purpose of the power is to become witnesses, to help others, to influence people for Christ; not to create superstars, test-market programs, employ fund-raising experts, and hold half-day services with television extravaganzas for the entertainment of Christians.

The mainline denominations see these abuses, and won't get in the car.

Few are using the car as transportation to the destination: to act in accordance with the Spirit of the Lord, to be "open on the God-ward side."

The church desperately needs individual members who are open on the God-ward side as a first-line ministry, as a priority, as a full serving of God, and without the flaky crust.

As J.B. Phillips says, *"Surely this is the church as it was meant to be...."*

> "It is impossible to spend several months in close study of the Acts of the Apostles, without being profoundly stirred and, to be honest, disturbed. The reader is stirred because he is seeing Christianity, the real thing, in action for the first time in human history....
>
> "Yet we cannot help feeling disturbed, as well as moved, *for this surely is the Church as it was meant to be.* It is vigorous and flexible, for these are the days before it ever became fat and short of breath through prosperity, or muscle-bound through over-organization. These men did not make acts of faith, they believed; they did not 'say their prayers', they really prayed. They did not hold conferences on psychosomatic medicine; they simply healed the sick. But if they were uncomplicated and naïve by modern standards we have ruefully to admit that *they were open on the God-ward side* in a way that is almost unknown today...."

"...the Spirit of God found what surely he must always be seeking—a fellowship of men and women so united in love and faith that he can work in them with the minimum of let (restraint) and hindrance. Consequently it is a matter of historical fact that never before has any small body of ordinary people so moved the world that their enemies could say, with tears of rage in their eyes, that these men 'have turned the world upside down.'"

"...Indeed, in exactly the same way as Jesus Christ in the flesh cut right through the matted layers of tradition and exposed the real issue;...so we find here the Spirit of Jesus dealing not so much with problems as with people."

—J.B. Phillips, *The Price of Success*, (italics mine throughout)

The Spirit of the Lord is still seeking those he can work through, with a "minimum of restraint and hindrance." Some of them are still around—can still hear God.

Chapter 25

. . . .

How Will It Be?

Few people had better reason to feel remorse and shame. Simon Peter had boasted to friends and companions about his bravery, loyalty, and closeness to a good friend. But he folded when the chips were down; he publicly betrayed and denied his friend. And now this friend whom he so treacherously treated has come back to confront him...

Get ready—the accusations are about to begin...

The friend was Jesus. The meeting, however, was different than Peter expected. Jesus makes no mention of the past; there is no mention of boasting or denial. Nothing is said about letting a friend down or betrayal. For Jesus, it's all about *relationship*: "Do you love me?"

We may have made serious mistakes. We may have denied the Lord we love. Shame and a sense of our future untrustworthiness may keep us from returning to him, being with him, serving him. This should never be. Jesus will always accept us. No finger pointing, no accusations, no recriminations, *no demotions*. He does not ask "Why?" He only asks, "Do you love me?"

123

The prodigal son returns. His admission of failure is cut short in mid-sentence; his father won't even let him complete it for the joy of seeing him. "We're not going to talk about failure; we're not going to talk about the past; it's passed. What's important is the love we have for each other *now*."

The past does have some value. We can learn from it, but we shouldn't dwell permanently in it. I can view the person who made those mistakes with humor and sadness. I can learn humility, feel more deeply other's hurts. I can finally realize that Jesus will never reject me, no matter what mistakes I make. These lessons I carry with me permanently.

But having learned from the past, I should move on; otherwise, my personal history becomes a preoccupation with my *self*: *I'm the most worthless person that ever lived, the most treacherous, most undependable* (now add "egotistical, self-centered, magnificent sinner," and you have the self in all its glory). *I am a supreme failure. No one does it better than me!*

Never was there a better reason for bypassing what needs to be fixed. Wallowing in the mire of past failures robs us of power. The voice of Satan sounds like, *Remember when you did...? You always mess things up....* There is no strength in those words, no motivation to try again. It's like tearing off the bandage; the wound will never heal. The wound of the past is always fresh, preoccupying, and becomes the reason for not trying to improve the future. It becomes the reason for not trying, period. The problem in understanding the past is compounded by the fact that we don't really *know* the past.

What we have, though, are fragments of the past glued together from our fear, inexperience, events and the interpretation of events over the years. The past exists only in memory and is unreliable in determining character and potential. We do the best we can. When we're young, we have only a small amount of "memory database" with which to compare happenings. Insignificant events have enormous importance because we have so little for comparison. Adults might not give a second thought to events that send chills of fear through a child.

When I was in the first grade, our school had an outside in-cinerator; kids loved to throw paper into the flames and watch it burn. An old codger janitor, no doubt afraid he'd get into trouble for allowing this, yelled, "Hey, you kids! Get away from there. I have your names! I'm going to report you to the principal!"

Well, of course he didn't know who we were or our names. But I was in the first grade. I was terrified. I went home for lunch and refused to go back to school. My folks said I wouldn't have to if I would tell them the reason. What happened? Wild horses were of no use; I was more scared of the janitor. I wasn't telling anyone. I went back, nothing happened, nobody but me remem-bered the incident, but I quavered all day waiting to be taken to the principal's office where the dreaded electric paddle was awaiting. Adults know the electric paddle is a dark, false rumor, and can put things into perspective; they have more experience, a broader and deeper database.

Unfairness hurts children more than we know. Some kids remember unfair treatment over a minor incident long into adult years; a finely developed sense of fairness is ingrained in us. C. S. Lewis refers to it as the ever-present inner law, the basis for every argument, the clue to the meaning of the universe.[1]

The past is not clearly known to us because we have so little to base it on. The proof of this is vastly differing reminiscences as adults concerning shared childhood events. Several children, brought up in the same household with the same parents and economic influences, will have three different versions of "the truth."

The past limits us, exerts a pressure on us, and we don't even really know the past.

Moreover, we have differing views of what the past means. In a long-term study of adult children of alcoholics, two brothers were interviewed. Their behavior and perceptions of life were at opposite ends of the spectrum. One brother was a chronic alcoholic, like his father; the other was a sober pillar of the community. In the follow-up study, each gave the same answer to the same question, reflecting two opposing positions:

125

Question: "With an alcoholic father, why do you think you turned out the way you did?"

Answer: "With a father like mine, what other choice did I have?"

Their answers, identical; their life choices, complete opposites.

God's truth is absolute and unchanging. Man's perception of truth is highly subjective.

A speaker, telling his personal story, made this point dramatically during a Twelve-Step Retreat. He had rebelled at having to write out in detail his life story as required by his sponsor, an "uneducated, unemployed actor." He himself was highly educated and, what's more, had been through years of analysis. "I've already told my psychiatrist everything! Why do I need to write out this 'inventory'?" When he read the story of his life, complete with all the people he had hurt, he was astounded. "I hadn't told my shrink anything! No wonder he couldn't help me. I told him what he needed to know! After all, I'm not paying someone a hundred dollars an hour to reject me ('Get out of my office, you filthy pervert!')" Truth about the past can be filtered to favor us, or tailored more precisely to match the way we want others to see us.

Many popular "flavors" of psychoanalysis promote the idea that because the past has been a mess (even if it wasn't), the reasons for a poor performance lie in failures of others to be all they should have been: *Parents, authority figures, siblings—anybody you can think of—they're the reason I'm the way I am. I've been formed and deformed, and now I can't re-form. The past dictates the future. Result? There is no hope. Everyone else is to blame. It all happened a long time ago—and everyone agrees you can't go back and change the past. It's the ideal excuse for underachievement, non-performance (and not sending out any Christmas cards). They did it: they're to blame. (It works for me!).*

Jesus makes it clear: relationships and fish dinners around the campfire—that's what's important. In that setting, we can talk about the future. *"Do you love me? Feed my sheep. Take care of my little ones; make sure they have enough to eat. Guide them; protect them as*

126

I would if I were there. Do you love me, Peter? The past isn't important to me, Peter. There's a big job ahead, and you're the man big enough for it. I have in mind a promotion, not a demotion. How 'bout it?"

No recriminations, no discussions of what went wrong. A mission awaits; a vision for the future unfolds. The church—something never before seen on the face of this earth—is being founded. The church is being entrusted to a fallible, yet strong human individual; a person with a past. *"You are Peter... the rock...my rock...and on this rock I will build my church, and the gates of hell will not hold out against it."*

God never consults your past to determine your future. He sees qualities no one else sees, and draws them out for the mission. The mission supersedes the past; the past is bypassed. The calling calls and brings new resources. It's the call that equips us; where God guides, God provides. The choice is clear: will the past dominate, or the future? Will partial impressions of past memories define my identity, my life from now on—or will "mission-mind"?

You decide.

Chapter 26

Grace Will
Lead Me Home

Grace has been defined in various ways. The Amplified Bible uses the phrase, "God's unmerited favor."[1] The one I like best is Brennan Manning's "accepted tenderness."

To know God better, we must first come to "know and rely on the love God has for us;"[2] that he loves us not as we should be, but as we are. We trust God just about as much as we love him, and we must learn to trust him if we want him to lead us, to guide us.

God's guidance does not mean certainty about a particular course of action, but rather certainty concerning his intentions toward us—that he will walk with us each step of the way, guiding us as we go.

I can trust God more fully if I am convinced of his love that is never based on my abilities or performance. God is drawn to me because of my need, not my perfection.

A man was asked which of his thirteen kids was his favorite. He named each one as his favorite, depending on which one needed him the most at any given time.

God is like that. The Good Shepherd loves the ninety and nine that are safe, but his longing and his search is for the one still lost, still in danger, still in the storm. Christianity is not about numbers, and never can be; size is not a moral quality. Like any good parent, God's concern is for the one still hurting.

The question then is not, "Do I think God loves me?" Most people with even a nodding acquaintance of the Bible would say, "Yes, I believe God loves me." The question that is now important is, "Do I believe that God *likes* me?" Often, the answer is, "How could he, knowing all that I have done and thought?"

Our sin will become our glory, not because it was good for us to have done those things, but because it will be a shining example of God's forgiveness. The apostle Paul quoted Jesus as saying, "My grace is sufficient for you, for my power is made perfect in weakness." Paul continues: "Therefore I will boast all the more gladly about my weaknesses, so that Christ's power may rest on me. That is why, for Christ's sake, I delight in weaknesses, in insults, in hardships, in persecutions, in difficulties. For when I am weak, then I am strong."[3]

God is not looking for perfect people; he is looking for people who know they're not. That's why the worst people—prostitutes, thieves, tax collectors—felt so loved and accepted in Jesus' presence. He wanted people to stop doing the things that damaged them and hurt others. He wanted them to know he loved them, felt "tenacious tenderness" towards them and, if they wanted, he would help them.

Sinners would become examples of his amazing grace; and he would lead them home to safety.

It is your need that draws God to you. And he will lead you safely home.

"*I speak in a poem of the ancient food of heroes: humiliation, unhappiness, discord. Those things were given to us to transform so that we may make from the miserable circumstances of our lives things that are eternal, or aspire to be so.*"

—Jorge Luis Borges

Endnotes

I am indebted to the many authors, teachers and writers listed here for their illustrative stories and examples. Every effort was made to trace these stories to their source. I hope I got it right.

Introduction
[1] Matthew 16:13; 15 LB
[2] Mark 10:18
[3] Luke 15:17-18. He was in the pigpen, he came to himself, and he said, "I will go home." (paraphrased)

Chapter 1: The Near End of God
[1] Adapted from Carl G. Carlozzi's "The Wayward Daughter," *Pocket Parables* (Illinois: Tyndale House, 1985), p. 107.
[2] Arthur Miller, *After the Fall, A Play in Two Acts*. Final stage version (New York: The Penguin Group, 1964), p. 22.
[3] Harry Emerson Fosdick, "Those Marvelous Twelve Steps," *AA Grapevine*, Volume 46, Issue 3, August 1989.
[4] Gertrude Behanna, "God Isn't Dead," original recording LP Word 3179 (1962), digital edition 2002 by www.aabibliography.com. Paraphrased for this chapter by the author.

[5] This story has many sources and occasions and is probably apocryphal. Tony Campola in his book, *Let Me Tell You a Story* locates the occasion at the University of Chicago.

Chapter 2: I Can't Do It
[1] Matthew 17:20
[2] Romans 8:26 Phillips

Chapter 3: Misfits
[1] 1 Samuel 22:2
[2] See 1 Corinthians 6:9-11.

Chapter 4: The Light Must Be Gentle
[1] I am indebted to Keith Miller for this example.
[2] Isaiah 42:3, Matthew 12:20
[3] J.B. Phillips, *The Price of Success: An Autobiography* (Illinois: Harold Shaw Publishers, 1984), p. 160.
[4] Saint Bernard of Clairvaux quoted in *The Soul Afire: Revelations of the Mystics*, H.A. Reinhold, ed. (New York: Image Books-Doubleday, 1973), p. 204.

Chapter 5: Grace Magnet
[1] Ephesians 3:19, 20

Chapter 6: The Power of Forgiveness
[1] See Matthew 6:14, 15

Chapter 7: Fear Management
[1] See Matthew 8:26, Matthew 14:27, Luke 8:50 for some examples.
[2] Dale Carnegie, *How to Stop Worrying and Start Living* (New York: Pocket Books-Simon & Schuster, 1984), p. 162, 163.
[3] Carnegie, *How to Stop Worrying*, p.163.
[4] Jeremiah 29:11
[5] Romans 8:31

Chapter 8: Pray As You Can, Not As You Can't
[1] Philippians 4:6-7, emphasis added.
[2] Phrase attributed to Dom John Chapman.
[3] *In The Garden*, text and music by C. Austin Miles, 1913. Public Domain.

[4] Madalene Harris "Bearing One Another's Burdens," from *How To Improve Your Prayer Life* (Missouri:Aldersgate Associates, 1987), Stephen M. Miller, ed., pgs. 52-54.

[5] 1 Thessalonians 5:17

[6] Brother Lawrence and Joseph de Beaufort, *The Practice of the Presence of God* (Pennsylvania: Whitaker House, 1982) p. 20.

[7] *Romero.* Director: John Duigan. Performers: Raul Julia, Richard Jordan, Ana Alicia. Paulist Pictures, 1989. The scene, in which the Salvadoran priest, Archbishop Oscar Romero (Raul Julia), prays the ultimate prayer of surrender and consecration.

Chapter 9: Wasteful Love
The account of Mary of Bethany is recorded in three of the four Gospels: Matthew 26:6-13; Mark 14:3-9; and Luke 7:36-50.

[1] The waste factor was significant in that the estimated value of the ointment was at least one year's wages. One Bible commentator estimates that the sale of this ointment would have fed the five thousand without the miracle of the loaves and the fishes.

Chapter 10: Carefully Careless
[1] David McCasland's, *Oswald Chambers: Abandoned To God* (Nashville: Discovery House, 1993), p. 225.

[2] McCasland, *Abandoned To God*, p. 194-195.

[3] Jeremiah 29:11

[4] McCasland, *Abandoned To God*, p. 177.

[5] Behanna, *God Isn't Dead.* See Chap. 1, n. 2.

[6] See Philippians 4:7.

[7] Proverbs 10:22

[8] Psalms 23:4

[9] Psalms 23:1

[10] McCasland, *Abandoned To God*, p. 188.

[11] McCasland, *Abandoned To God*, p. 118.

[12] McCasland, *Abandoned To God*, p. 225.

[13] McCasland, *Abandoned To God*, p. 190.

[14] McCasland, *Abandoned To God*, p. 276.

Chapter 11: The Mystery of the Wounded Healer
[1] Matthew 27:42 KJV

[2] Robert Coles, "The Inexplicable Prayers of Ruby Bridges" from *Finding God at Harvard: Spiritual Journeys of Thinking Christians*, Kelly Monroe, ed. (Michigan: Zondervan Publishing House, 1996), pg. 38.
[3] Mark 9:29 (paraphrased)
[4] Henri J.M. Nouwen, *The Wounded Healer* (New York: An Image Book-Doubleday, 1972), p. 88.

Chapter 12: Holy Motivation
[1] Romans 4:3
[2] 1 John 4:16
[3] Phrase attributed to Brennan Manning.
[4] C.S. Lewis, *The Letters of C.S. Lewis*, p. 285, Letter dated April 29, 1959.
[5] Edwin Robertson, *The Shame and the Sacrifice: the Life and Martyrdom of Dietrich Bonhoeffer* (New York: Collier Books-Macmillan Publishing Co., 1988), p. 174 (emphasis added).
[6] Charles W. Colson, *Born Again* (New Jersey: Revell Company, 1977), p. 134. (Doug Coe's inscription in the Phillips New Testament given to Charles Colson, founder of Prison Fellowship, when Colson was a new Christian).

Chapter 13: Spaces
[1] Luke 4:42
[2] Galen Guengerich, from his sermon *Wide Margins*. May, 1999.
[3] Henry David Thoreau, "Life Without Principle" lectures appearing in *Walden and Other Writings*, edited by Brooks Atkinson (New York: Random House, 1992), pg. 764.

Chapter 14: ¿Para Hoy?
[1] Matthew 6:34 KJV
[2] Carnegie, p. 3. See Chap. 7, n. 1.
[3] Carnegie, p. 10. See Chap. 7, n. 1.

Chapter 15: More Certain Joys
[1] Statement made by Napolean at Saint Helena. Carnegie, p. 121. See Chap. 7, n. 1.
[2] See Chapter 13, n. 2.
[3] See Ecclesiastes 3:1-8 KJV.
[4] Charles McCarry, *Citizen Nader* (New York: Signet, 1972), p. 37.
[5] Robert C. Buckhorn, *The People's Lawyer* (Prentice-Hall,1972).

Chapter 16: A Time For Everything
Quote by Dr. Martin Luther King, Jr., taken from his sermon entitled "The Death of Evil Upon the Seashore" published in *Strength to Love* (New York: Harper & Row, 1963).
[1] Psalms 104:15
[2] Percy Bysshe Shelley, *Ozymandias*, first published 1817.

Chapter 17: In This World
[1] *Shadowlands*. Director: Richard Attenborough. Performers: Anthony Hopkins, Debra Winger, Edward Hardwicke. Spelling Films/Warner Bros.,1994.
[2] Anne Lamott, *Traveling Mercies, Some Thoughts On Faith* (Anchor Books, 1999).

Chapter 18: Notes From Home
[1] Matthew 11:12 AMP
[2] Romans 13:10 LB
[3] Luke 12:32 KJV
[4] See Psalms 37:4.

Chapter 19: Stop Loss Orders
[1] Psalm 1:1
[2] *Dilbert* © 2004 United Feature Syndicate, Inc.

Chapter 20: Not a Bribe, A Belonging
[1] 2 Corinthians 9:7
[2] Luke 6:38
[3] Luke 6:38

Chapter 21: The Royal Law...Love Myself?
[1] 1 Corinthians 13: 4-7 LB
[2] "Do not call anything impure that God has made clean." Acts 10:15.

Chapter 22: Safe Within the Circle
[1] Psalms 23 LB
[2] See Acts 13:22.
[3] See Matthew 4:1-11 or Luke 4:1-13.
[4] See Luke 18:27.
[5] See John 5:19.
[6] Psalms 23:5 KJV

Chapter 23: Highest Honor

[1] James Ford Rhodes *History of the Civil War, 1861-1865* (New York: Macmillan Company, 1917; New York: Bartleby.com, 2000), pg. 246.

Chapter 24: Open on the God-ward Side

[1] Soren Kirkegaard, *Purity of Heart is to Will One Thing* (Harper, 1938).
[2] J.B. Phillips, *The Price of Success: An Autobiography* (Illinois: Harold Shaw, 1984), p. 159.
[3] Acts 1:8 Phillips (emphasis mine)

Chapter 25: How Will It Be?

Jesus' dialogue with Peter drawn from Matthew 16: 18 and John 21: 15-17.
[1] See "Right and Wrong as a Clue to the Meaning of the Universe", chapter 1: The Law of Human Nature from *Mere Christianity* by C.S. Lewis (New York: Macmillan, 1943).

Chapter 26: Grace Will Lead Me Home

[1] Ephesians 2:8 AMP
[2] 1 John 4:16
[3] 2 Corinthians 12: 8-10

To order additional copies of

Have your credit card ready and call:

1-877-421-READ (7323)

or please visit our web site at
www.pleasantword.com

Also available at:
www.amazon.com
and
www.barnesandnoble.com

Printed in the United States
78168LV00007B/25-54